JERRY SAVELLE

Why God Wants You to Prosper

Published by Jerry Savelle Ministries
Crowley, Texas, U.S.A.
www.jerrysavelle.org

Unless otherwise noted, Scripture quotations are taken from the New King James Version ®. Copyright © 1982 by Thomas Nelson, Inc. Used by permission. All rights reserved.

KJV — *King James Version.* Authorized King James Version.

NIV — THE HOLY BIBLE, NEW INTERNATIONAL VERSION®, NIV® Copyright © 1973, 1978, 1984, 2011 by Biblica, Inc.® Used by permission. All rights reserved worldwide.

AMP — THE AMPLIFIED BIBLE, Old Testament copyright © 1965, 1987 by the Zondervan Corporation. The Amplified New Testament copyright © 1958, 1987 by the Lockman Foundation. Used by permission.

TLB — The Living Bible copyright © 1971 by Tyndale House Foundation. Used by permission of Tyndale House Publishers Inc., Carol Stream, Illinois 60188. All rights reserved. The Living Bible, TLB, and the The Living Bible logo are registered trademarks of Tyndale House Publishers.

Lamsa Scripture quotation is from the Holy Bible From Ancient Eastern Manuscripts, George M. Lamsa, Copyright © 1933, 1939, 1940, 1957 A. J. Holman Company.

© 2014 Jerry Savelle Ministries
All rights reserved.

ISBN 978-1-939934-00-0

Rights for publishing this book outside the U.S.A or in non-English languages are administered by Jerry Savelle Ministries, an international not-for-profit ministry. For additional information, please visit jerrysavelle.org, or email info@jsmi.org, or write to

Jerry Savelle Ministries, PO Box 748, Crowley, TX 76036, U.S.A.

To order copies of this book and other resources in bulk quantities,
please contact us at 1-817-297-3155.

Table of Contents

Introduction IV

   Part One: Understanding the Principles of Divine Prosperity

Chapter 1 Prosperity Is God's Will for Us. 3

Chapter 2 Knowledge and Wisdom Produce Prosperity 19

Chapter 3 The Purpose of Prosperity 43

Chapter 4 Spirit-led Giving Produces the Fruits of Righteousness . 61

Chapter 5 Why God's People Are in Financial Bondage 71

   Part Two: Keys to a Lifestyle of Walking in Prosperity

Chapter 6 Develop a Lifestyle of Obedience 93

Chapter 7 Develop a Lifestyle of Faith. 107

Chapter 8 Develop a Lifestyle of Giving. 127

Chapter 9 Develop a Lifestyle of Pursuing God 145

Chapter 10 A Call to Action 161

Introduction

I remember the evening in 1969 as if it happened only yesterday. I was new to the ministry and had just delivered a sermon declaring that, not only were our days of sickness over because of the redemptive work Jesus accomplished on the cross, but also that His redemptive work freed us from poverty—spirit, soul, body, and financially. I told of the miracles God had done in my life and in the lives of others who'd dared to believe God's Word and act on it.

As I stepped down from the platform after my closing prayer, I was startled when a large man appeared out of nowhere, grabbed my collar, and nearly lifted me from the floor.

"I want to tell you something," he said, looking as if the vein on his forehead was about to pop. "I don't like your message one bit. I spent four years of my life in the seminary studying God's Word, but instead of preaching, I'm now selling life insurance just to pay my debts. You've never spent one day in the seminary, yet you're out here preaching, and God is doing miracles. I'm not seeing God move like that in my life—and I want to know why."

My answer to him was short and direct: "Sir, if you've been to seminary, then you know a lot about the Bible, and that's a good thing. But the reason God is doing miracles in my life is simple: I'm *living* the Bible."

My statement about living the Bible was true then, and it's still true after more than forty years. My wife, Carolyn, and I have taken to heart these words of the Bible: "Beloved, I pray that you may prosper in all things and be in health, just as your soul prospers" (3 John 2).

So we understand from reading 3 John 2 that health and prosperity are God's will for our lives; Christ has redeemed us from sickness and poverty. Because Carolyn and I have chosen to live what we believe, we have enjoyed good physical health throughout the years and continue to prosper and succeed in every area of our lives—spirit, soul, and body. Our ministry is also prospering and debt free, and we attribute all of this to the faithfulness of our God.

What began with one young couple armed with nothing more than a desire to get out of debt and a bold faith in the integrity of the Word of God has become a thriving ministry organization that is reaching the world with the gospel of Jesus Christ. In addition to establishing a vibrant local church, Heritage of Faith Christian Center in Crowley, Texas, Jerry Savelle Ministries International has offices on four continents. Our television broadcast is aired worldwide, and our teachings are distributed via print and electronic media.

While faith in God's Word is the foundation on which we've based our life and ministry, in the natural it takes an astounding amount of money to accomplish all God has called us to do in this day and hour. When God speaks to us about something He wants done, we must be able to do it quickly, without hesitation or hindrance, and without having to consult others. In Paul's letter to the church in Corinth, he says the result of God's grace in our lives is that we "may always and under all circumstances and whatever the need, be self-sufficient—possessing enough to require no aid or support and furnished in abundance for every good work and charitable donation" (2 Corinthians 9:8 AMP).

In other words, God's purpose for prospering us is not just that our own needs may be met but that He might use us to be a blessing to others.

Being "self-sufficient" and "furnished in abundance" means we must be free from the crippling bondage of debt. Prosperity and bondage cannot coexist. It has never been God's will for His people to be in bondage of any kind. When Christians lose sleep wondering how they are going to pay their bills, that's a pretty good indication they are in financial bondage. I know, because that's exactly where I was at one time.

Carolyn and I had been living in debt for years, struggling just to keep up with the interest payments on what we owed. I actually believed the only way to get the material things I needed was to borrow money and then make payments to the lender. That's what my dad had done all of his life, and it's what I'd learned to do. The Bible says, "The borrower is servant to the lender" (Proverbs 22:7), and that's just what Carolyn and I were: servants.

But there came a time when we had to make a stand and start living by the Word of God. It wasn't so much a major decision on our part; it's just that we were broke and the bank wouldn't loan us any more money. We saw in the Bible that poverty and lack were part of the curse and that the people's disobedience opened the door to the curse. However, when God's people chose to obey His Word, then they lived under the cover of His blessing.

Carolyn and I began to obey the Word of God where our money was concerned, and God began performing miracles in our finances. It didn't happen overnight, but eventually we were completely delivered out of our debt. And I have to tell you that after experiencing both the bondage of debt and the freedom of prosperity, I'll take prosperity any day.

Sadly, there are still many Christians who are not yet experiencing the blessing of prosperity that has been provided for them. Some are on the verge of financial disaster, facing foreclosure and loss of businesses. Others are caught in a never-ending struggle with their financial obligations, finding themselves with little left over each month after covering their debt payments. Then there are those who are "furnished in abundance," as we read in 2 Corinthians, yet they've never known the peace, quietness, and confidence that come from allowing God to direct the use of their finances for His purposes. They don't realize they are just as much in financial bondage as those who suffer lack.

But the good news is that God has already provided the way out of financial bondage and into prosperity—if we are just willing to obey His instructions. The reason I've written this two-part book is to share with you what I've learned over more than forty years in ministry about why God wants us to prosper. The material contained in part one will give you a clear understanding of the biblical principles relating to divine prosperity, while part two contains the keys to walking in that prosperity. You'll also read personal accounts of my own journey to walking in prosperity, including the supernatural revelation I received from the Lord about freeing His people financially.

When the disciples asked Jesus what would be the sign of His coming and of the end of the age, He said, "And this gospel of the kingdom will be preached in all the world as a witness to all the nations, and then the end will come" (Matthew 24:14).

My friend, we've reached the place on God's timetable that we can no longer be dependent upon the financial system of this world. Our heavenly Father wants us to possess the goods of this world for one reason: to make them available to Him to be used so that the gospel of the kingdom will be preached in all the world.

Part One
Understanding the Principles of Divine Prosperity

Chapter 1
Prosperity Is God's Will for Us

From the time God blessed the first man and woman, commissioning them to "be fruitful and multiply; fill the earth and subdue it; have dominion over the fish of the sea, over the birds of the air, and over every living thing that moves on the earth" (Genesis 1:28), it was His will that they prosper, or succeed, in everything they did.

Although Adam and Eve had no need of money to fulfill this commission, God knew that mankind would one day need to establish a monetary system to ensure continued prosperity and social order in the advancement of His kingdom. That's why He made a deposit of wealth within the earth. Near the Garden of Eden was a land called Havilah. The Bible says it is a place "where there is gold. And the gold of that land is good. Bdellium and the onyx stone are there" (Genesis 2:11–12).

We don't know if Abraham ever patronized the First National Bank of Havilah. But we do know that because God chose him as the man through whom He would establish His covenant in the earth, he was a prosperous and wealthy man, In fact, the Bible says, "Abram was very rich in livestock, in silver, and in gold" (Genesis 13:2).

When God delivered His people out of the bondage of slavery in Egypt to serve Him only, in addition to going out with flocks and herds of livestock, they took with them great wealth: "Now the children of Israel had done according to the word of Moses, and they had asked from the Egyptians articles of silver, articles of gold, and clothing. And the LORD had given the people favor in the sight of the Egyptians, so that they granted them what they requested. Thus they plundered the Egyptians" (Exodus 12:35–36).

As Joshua was about to lead God's people across the Jordan River into their inheritance, a land described as flowing with milk and honey, God made this promise: "As I was with Moses, so I will be with you. I will not leave you nor forsake you. Be strong and of good courage, for to this people you shall divide as an inheritance the land which I swore to their fathers to give them. Only be strong and very courageous, that you may observe to do according to all the law which Moses My servant commanded you; do not turn from it to the right hand or to the left, that you may prosper wherever you go" (Joshua 1:5–7).

In each of the instances above, God commissioned either selected individuals or groups of people to carry out specific assignments. And in each instance God saw to it that they prospered. It was His way of ensuring the success of each assignment. So if God was so committed in Old Testament times to seeing His people prosper, or succeed, in what He had called them to do, doesn't it stand to reason that prosperity is also His will for us under the New Covenant?

When Jesus appeared to His disciples after completing His redemptive work on the cross, He gave this commission: "Go into all the world and preach the gospel to every creature" (Mark 16:15). The disciples were aware that this task had to be completed before Jesus could return, because He'd already told them what was to happen (see Matthew 24:14). But how could eleven men, who had to either walk or ride donkeys to get where they were going, ever accomplish such a feat? They couldn't at the time, but with today's technology and transportation capabilities—we can!

As Christ's representatives and ambassadors in this world, we have been given the awesome and exciting responsibility of taking part in the worldwide preaching of the gospel that must be accomplished before His return. There is an enormous job to be done, and to accomplish this job we need to be prosperous and funded.

You may be thinking, "I believe prosperity is God's will for me, but how is it going to happen in my life? I wasn't born into wealth; I'm just an average person with an average job, trying to pay the mortgage and take care of my family."

There was a time when I wondered the same thing myself. I couldn't figure out how God could possibly use a guy who owned a paint and body shop, and was just barely getting by, to help take His gospel to the world. But then I read Proverbs 13:22, which says, "The wealth of the sinner is laid up for the righteous." That sounded like good news to me, and I liked it even better when I read the Amplified version: "The wealth of the sinner [finds its way eventually] into the hands of the righteous, for whom it was laid up."

It may look like the devil is in control of the world's wealth, what with unemployment being higher than it's been in decades and many nations on the brink of economic collapse. But we do not have to be affected by the world's system. The Bible gives us this assurance:

> What then shall we say to these things? If God is for us, who can be against us? He who did not spare His own Son, but delivered Him up for us all, how shall He not with Him also freely give us all things? Who shall bring a charge against God's elect? It is God who justifies. Who is he who condemns? It is Christ who died, and furthermore is also risen, who is even at the right hand of God, who also makes intercession for us. Who shall separate us from the love of Christ? Shall tribulation, or distress, or persecution, or famine, or nakedness, or peril, or sword? As it is written:
>
> > "For Your sake we are killed all day long; We
> > are accounted as sheep for the slaughter."
>
> Yet in all these things we are more than conquerors through Him who loved us. For I am persuaded that neither death nor life, nor angels nor principalities nor powers, nor things present nor things to come, nor height nor depth, nor any other created thing, shall be able to separate us from the love of God which is in Christ Jesus our Lord (Romans 8:31–39).

It is vital to understand that, in His great love for us, God has not promised to freely give us all things, as we read above, just to squander on our own pleasures. While He is not against our possessing things, He doesn't want those things to possess us. When we allow material objects to capture our time and attention, we risk becoming distracted from the work God has called us to do, and we are therefore subject to falling into error. He loves us too much to allow this to happen, and we can count on Him to correct us when we need it, as it says in the book of Job:

> When we allow material objects to capture our time and attention, we risk becoming distracted from the work God has called us to do, and we are therefore subject to falling into error.

> Then He shows to them [the true character of] their deeds and their transgressions, that they have acted arrogantly [with presumption and self-sufficiency].
> He also opens their ears to instruction and discipline, and commands that they return from iniquity.
> If they obey and serve Him, they shall spend their days in prosperity and their years in pleasantness and joy (Job 36:9–11 AMP).

If we will keep our hearts pure before God, He will show us where we are in error. Error creates bondage and prevents the flow of His prosperity into our lives, but Jesus said the truth will set us free (see John 8:32). That's why, as members of the Body of Christ, we should welcome correction from the Lord. I've come to realize that when I'm in error, the best thing God can do for me is tell me plainly, "Jerry, here's the problem." Sometimes this kind of revelation hurts, but it's better than living in bondage—especially financial bondage.

It is God's will that we prosper in every area of our lives as He accomplishes His will and purpose in and through us. If we want to tap into the wealth that has been laid up for us to use in accomplishing these purposes, we need to welcome God's correction and instruction.

Prosperity Is a Redemptive Truth

I've never understood why people argue about something God has given us. For instance, I've heard some say, "Our pastor says healing has passed away and that the prosperity message comes from a cult." I'm glad nobody told Abraham that; otherwise, he might have died young and never received all those riches from God.

Prosperity is a redemptive truth, just as physical health is a redemptive truth. This truth was first established within the blessing God conferred on mankind in the garden: to be fruitful, to multiply, to fill the earth, to subdue it, and to have dominion. There was no sickness, poverty, or bondage to sin in the garden; life in communion with God was productive and perfect—that is, until Satan launched his plan of deception and mankind fell into sin through disobedience.

But God also had a plan. Instead of leaving mankind to suffer in a fallen condition, He sent His own Son, Jesus Christ, to pay the debt for sin and restore all who would receive His redemption into relationship with their heavenly Father. The redemptive work Jesus accomplished on the cross restored the health, prosperity, and freedom that God had conferred upon mankind in the garden. In other words, anything that belonged to mankind in the garden is a redemptive truth that Jesus restored at the cross.

Jesus made a bold statement about this redemptive work one Sabbath day in Nazareth. The Bible says it was His custom to read in the synagogue, but this day something was different in the way He delivered God's Word.

> The redemptive work Jesus accomplished on the cross restored the health, prosperity, and freedom that God had conferred upon mankind in the garden.

And He was handed the book of the prophet Isaiah. And when He had opened the book, He found the place where it was written:

> "The Spirit of the LORD is upon Me, because He has anointed Me to preach the gospel to the poor; He has sent Me to heal the brokenhearted, to proclaim liberty to the captives and recovery of sight to the blind, to set at liberty those who are oppressed; to proclaim the acceptable year of the LORD."

Then He closed the book, and gave it back to the attendant and sat down. And the eyes of all who were in the synagogue were fixed on Him. And He began to say to them, "Today this Scripture is fulfilled in your hearing" (Luke 4:17–21).

Here we see Jesus proclaiming that God had anointed Him to preach the gospel to the poor. In this case, *poor* can mean poor in spirit, poor in soul, poor in body, poor financially, or poor socially.

There are many people who are poor in some area of their lives; some are poor in every area. Regardless of the circumstances, the gospel is for the poor. If you are poor in any area of your life, whether it be physically, socially, or financially, God has something He wants to say to you. He has a redemptive truth to cover every aspect of your life.

I don't know about you, but I'm tired of the world telling me how everything is going to turn out. I made up my mind long ago not to let the newspaper, online reports, or the evening news predict my destiny. As for me and my house, we will listen to what God has to say. I've learned that when we listen to what God says and are obedient to follow His instructions, then we don't have to be poor in any area of our lives.

Through the prophet Isaiah, God said, "For My thoughts are not your thoughts, nor are your ways My ways … For as the heavens are higher than the earth, so are My ways higher than your ways, and My thoughts than your thoughts" (Isaiah 55:8–9). Some people use this scripture to justify their position that God's ways are past finding out. But they are wrong. We have God's Word and we have the Teacher, the Holy Spirit, who indwells us for the purpose of leading us into all truth. The Bible says, "Now we have received, not the spirit of the world, but the Spirit who is from God, that we might know the things that have been freely given to us by God" (1 Corinthians 2:12).

> I've learned that when we listen to what God says and are obedient to follow His instructions, then we don't have to be poor in any area of our lives.

We are not in the dark; we know who we are in Christ and what is ours through His redemptive work on the cross. And because the Holy Spirit indwells us, then God's ways can become our ways and His thoughts can be our thoughts. As far as the world knows, there is no hope for financial prosperity and security anymore. The Bible says that people who are without God are without hope (see Ephesians 2:12). People without hope don't know the outcome of anything; they don't know what's going to happen tomorrow.

You may say, "I'm a Christian, and I don't know that." Well, you should know it. I don't mean to say it's possible to know every detail of your life, but you can know this: "No weapon formed against you shall prosper" (Isaiah 54:17); "if God is for [you], who can be against [you]?" (Romans 8:31); and, best of all, nothing "shall be able to separate [you] from the love of God which is in Christ Jesus [your] Lord" (Romans 8:39).

The world is suffering today. Governments are failing and financial institutions are not working. I can't remember the last time I heard a positive report about the financial situation in this country. For the most part, this mess we're in is because carnally minded people have ignored the godly principles upon which this nation was founded. But the good news is, where sin abounds, grace abounds all the more (see Romans 5:20). Jesus said, "Now when these things begin to happen, look up and lift up your heads, because your redemption draws near" (Luke 21:28).

Our prosperity—spirit, soul, and body—is a redemptive truth that we can count on.

We Don't Have to Live According to the Beggarly Elements of This World

There was once a time in my life when I was so broke that I literally didn't have enough money to buy lunch when I was at work. I was so in debt that I couldn't see a way things would ever change. But then I found out I didn't have to be poor. The Bible says, "For you know the grace of our Lord Jesus Christ, that though He was rich, yet for your sakes He became poor, that you through His poverty might become rich" (2 Corinthians 8:9).

I learned that there was a higher way to live financially, above what the Bible calls "the beggarly elements of the world" (see Galatians 4:9). I looked up the definition of the word *poor*, as used in the New Testament, in my Strong's Concordance and it literally means "begging; destitute; helpless; lacking." It was not God's intent in the beginning that His people should live like beggarly and helpless paupers, and it's not His intent that we live this way now—especially after He sent Jesus to preach the gospel to the poor.

Despite the fact that prosperity is a redemptive truth, there are those who reject this message because they have seen it abused by people who have set their eyes on nothing but the things money can buy. Such people are focused not on an intimate relationship with God; instead they are consumed with the desire to fulfill the lust of the eye and the flesh—and to do it in the name of faith. They have distorted the truth, and in so doing, their actions have done a great injustice to God's Word and a great disservice to His people.

There are other people whose hearts are right and pure before God, and He is prospering them. Rather than condemning them for their prosperity, we should learn from them. The Bible tells us to be "followers of them who through faith and patience inherit the promises" (Hebrews 6:12 KJV). The more we prosper, the more we can do for our God.

We must be careful not to reject the truth of God's Word because some people have misinterpreted, distorted, or abused that truth. All false teaching is based on the truth of Scripture, which has subsequently been distorted. God wants us saved, filled with His Spirit, set free from the bondage of sin, healed, and prosperous. He has made this gift available to us through the redemptive work Jesus did on the cross. But it's our choice to take it or leave it. I recommend taking it—all of it—because Jesus paid such a precious price for it.

Earlier in this chapter we read the account in Luke 4:18 of Jesus quoting out loud the words of Isaiah, saying, "I am anointed to preach the gospel to the poor." In essence, what He was telling those gathered that day in the synagogue was, "In these writings by Isaiah, the prophet was not speaking of himself, but of One to come. I am the One."

You'd think everyone would have rejoiced at that news—especially the Jews. Here was the promised Messiah, the One of whom the prophets had spoken of, the One who would deliver them, the One who would set up His kingdom and reign. They had been waiting for Him for centuries, and now here He was, standing in their midst. Yet what they heard did not sound like good news to them. In fact, what Jesus said made them so mad they wanted to kill Him.

> So all those in the synagogue, when they heard these things, were filled with wrath, and rose up and thrust Him out of the city; and they led Him to the brow of the hill on which their city was built, that they might throw Him down over the cliff. Then passing through the midst of them, He went His way (Luke 4:28–30).

Why didn't they want to hear the good news? Because their minds had been blinded. The eyes of their understanding were not enlightened. Simply put, they couldn't get past their religious tradition. And let me tell you something I've learned over the years: religious tradition always seeks to keep people living according the beggarly elements of this world. Take, for instance, the "vow of poverty," considered by some to represent the height of purity, which is taken when entering certain religious orders. Why would someone want to take a traditional vow of poverty when Jesus has redeemed us from poverty?

The number one reason people can't let go of their religious traditions is pride. In addition, some ministers today will not let go of teachings that are contrary to God's Word because those teachings are agreeable with their denominations or traditions.

Sadly, people living today in our Western culture are not that different from those living in Jesus' day and culture. When Jesus proclaimed, "The Spirit of the LORD is upon Me, because He has anointed Me to preach the gospel to the poor; He has sent Me to heal the brokenhearted, to proclaim liberty to the captives and recovery of the sight to the blind, to set at liberty those who are oppressed; to proclaim the acceptable year of the LORD" (Luke 4:18–19), every person in that congregation who was poor, brokenhearted, captive, or blind should have rejoiced. But they didn't. They were angered by His message, and they rebelled against it. They decided it certainly couldn't be God's way of doing things because it went against their religious tradition. The same thing happens today when religious tradition is confronted with redemptive truth: people get mad.

But Jesus doesn't get mad. When people get mad and refuse to believe, He doesn't just say, "Let's forget it, Father. These human beings are a waste of our time. We've made a mistake." Do you know what Jesus does today? He simply takes His message elsewhere, just as He did then. The Bible says He went to Capernaum, where the people didn't have any better sense than to believe the good news. They didn't argue with Him, and as a result, miracles took place. Signs and wonders occurred as the power of God manifested in their midst. They believed the incarnate Word of God, and they were set free.

I remember the mighty move of God that took place among Catholics during the 1960s. These precious believers were being filled with the Holy Spirit and immersing themselves in the Word of God. Miracles were happening all around them.

Do you know what many of the so-called full gospel people were doing while this was happening? Unaware that revival was already going on all around them, they were praying, "Oh, God, send us revival." During that period, I remember preaching in one particular church where we experienced a tremendous move of God's Spirit. Afterward, the pastor said to me, "I haven't seen anything like this in fifteen years. I don't know why God hasn't moved like this since then." I thought, "Lord, this man has tunnel vision; he needs to get out of here and take a look at what's happening."

> No one can stop God from prospering His people, because prosperity has been God's will for us from the beginning. But the choice to receive that prosperity is entirely ours.

Jesus was God's messenger of the gospel (which means "good news") during His day, and we have been commissioned to be His messengers of the good news today. Just as it was in Jesus' day, there are people who do not want to hear the good news because they don't believe it. While unbelief cannot stop a move of God, it will certainly prevent a person from receiving what God has for them—including the prosperity we so desperately need to accomplish His will.

No one can stop God from prospering His people, because prosperity has been God's will for us from the beginning. But the choice to receive that prosperity is entirely ours. Speaking from personal experience, I highly recommend doing so.

Chapter 2
Knowledge and Wisdom Produce Prosperity

Do you realize that unregenerate mankind—carnally minded people—and God are diametrically opposed to each other? In other words, the world has one way of doing things; God has another. All you have to do is listen to any of the mass communication media available today, and you'll hear the world's way loud and clear.

While we can certainly obtain factual information from these communication media, the only viable source of truth remains the Word of God. The Bible says, "All Scripture is given by inspiration of God, and is profitable for doctrine, for reproof, for correction, for instruction in righteousness, that the man of God may be complete, thoroughly equipped for every good work" (2 Timothy 3:16–17).

Anytime God commissions us to accomplish a task for Him, it is His responsibility to see to it that we are thoroughly equipped for every good work. In other words, He will give us both the knowledge and wisdom we need in order to succeed.

God said, "My people are destroyed for lack of knowledge" (Hosea 4:6). There's no excuse for a lack of knowledge in the day and age in which we live. The Word of God is going forth throughout the world like never before via print, electronic media, and the Internet; therefore, the Body of Christ should have great knowledge of the things of God.

God has given us His Word, the Bible, and He's given us the Holy Spirit, the Spirit of Truth, who will guide us into all truth (see John 16:13). All the seals have been taken off God's Word. The Holy Spirit is revealing to us the inner workings of our covenant with God and showing us how to live by it—*if* we will listen and obey. The choice is ours:

> "If they obey and serve Him, they shall spend their days in prosperity, and their years in pleasures. But if they do not obey, they shall perish by the sword, and they shall die without **knowledge**" (Job 36:11–12, bold added).

Sadly, many members of the Body of Christ have fallen into the trap of going along with what the world says. If the world says there is a depression, the Body accepts it as truth and joins the world in wallowing in misery. Or if inflation is reported to be at an all-time high, the Body is only too happy to open the door to fretting and fear.

We should never accept what the world declares to be the truth; it may be factual, but it is *not* the truth.

Anytime someone asks me what I think about the depression, inflation, or whatever the economic disaster of the moment may be, I simply say, "I'm not participating."

"What do you mean, you're not participating? Don't you have any knowledge of how bad things are out there?"

"I know what it looks like, but I have a different kind of knowledge," I tell them as I point to the Word of God:

> Anytime someone asks me what I think about the depression, inflation, or whatever the economic disaster of the moment may be, I simply say, "I'm not participating."

> Grace and peace be multiplied to you in the **knowledge** of God and of Jesus our Lord, as His divine power has given to us all things that pertain to life and godliness, through the **knowledge** of Him who called us by glory and virtue, by which have been given to us exceedingly great and precious promises, that through these you may be partakers of the divine nature, having escaped the corruption that is in the world through lust (2 Peter 1:2–4, bold added).

Just having knowledge of God and His ways alone does not ensure our success or our prosperity. We also need God's wisdom, which has to do with the correct and timely application of the knowledge He has given us. King Solomon, a man who prospered greatly through God's knowledge and wisdom, said, "The excellence of knowledge is that wisdom gives life to those who have it" (Ecclesiastes 7:12).

The Bible says there are two kinds of wisdom, *worldly* and *godly*. James describes worldly wisdom as "earthly, sensual, and demonic" (James 3:15). However, he goes on to say, "The wisdom that is from above is first pure, then peaceable, gentle, willing to yield, full of mercy and good fruits, without partiality and without hypocrisy" (James 3:17).

While worldly wisdom is something developed over time, godly wisdom is ours for the asking: "If any of you lacks wisdom, let him ask of God, who gives to all liberally and without reproach, and it will be given to him" (James 1:5). The Bible says wisdom actually calls out to us:

> Wisdom calls aloud outside; she raises her voice in the open squares. She cries out in the chief concourses, at the openings of the gates in the city she speaks her words: "How long, you simple ones, will you love simplicity? For scorners delight in their scorning, and fools hate knowledge. Turn at my rebuke; surely I will pour out my spirit on you; I will make my words known to you" (Proverbs 1:20–23).

The world's way of achieving prosperity is different from God's way. Although toiling was not God's original intent for mankind, it has been this way since Adam and Eve's act of disobedience in the garden when they fell out of spiritual union with God. The ground became cursed, and God said, "In toil you shall eat of it all the days of your life" (Genesis 3:17). As a result of the fall, man no longer enjoyed the peaceful and prosperous life of tending the garden God had created for him. Instead, he would toil and sweat all the days of his life just to produce bread.

In order to prosper in today's world, people generally engage in physical or mental work to meet their needs. The average American currently works 107 days—nearly one-third of the year—just to pay taxes. This is how the world's system works.

We may be *in* this world, but Jesus said we are not *of* it (see John 15:19). Therefore, we are not subject to this world's system. I'm not saying that we shouldn't have jobs. I'm saying our attitude about why we work should be different from the world's attitude. Paul said in Ephesians 4:28 of the King James Version that the believer applies "working with his hands the thing which is good, that he may have to give to him that needeth." We work so we will have seed to sow. We don't "work for a living"; we "work for a giving." When we choose to seek God's wisdom for every aspect of our lives, we are assured of the following blessings:

> Happy is the man who finds wisdom, and the man who gains understanding; for her proceeds are better than the profits of silver, and her gain than fine gold…Length of days is in her right hand, and in her left hand riches and honor (Proverbs 3:13–14, 16).

We belong to a higher order of living than the world's standard. We are to enjoy a prosperous life, not through sweat and toil, but through the knowledge and wisdom of God. Nevertheless, while

> "We are to enjoy a prosperous life, not through sweat and toil, but through the knowledge and wisdom of God."

length of days, riches, and honor already belong to us, many of God's children are not enjoying all of the benefits of this higher order of living. They have not yet made the decision to get into God's Word and find the godly knowledge and wisdom that produce prosperous living.

It takes determination to spend time in God's Word. At some point in our lives we each have to draw a line in the sand and declare, "In the name of Jesus, I'm not going to live the way the world lives anymore." This is not the easiest decision we will ever make, but I can promise that it's worth it. It's worth all the hours spent in God's Word and in fellowship with Him. It's worth the effort and the discipline it takes to refuse to go the world's way. It's worth it because, one day, payday will most certainly come. When we've tapped into the prosperous life that comes through godly knowledge and wisdom, we won't even consider going another way.

I can't imagine turning my back on God's way of living and returning to the way I used to live. God is prospering me, and I am blessed. I have divine health, and I'm enjoying the time of my life. I'm not saying I never have problems or that I never face adversity. If anything, I face greater adversity now than ever because the Bible says, "For everyone to whom much is given, from him much will be required" (Luke 12:48).

Knowledge and Wisdom Produce Prosperity

The devil does not stop attacking just because we have gained knowledge and wisdom. On the contrary, when we become more dangerous to him, he will attack even harder. But the Bible tells us exactly what to do when he attacks: "Therefore, submit to God. Resist the devil and he will flee from you" (James 4:7). The more knowledge and wisdom we have, the stronger we become. The stronger we become, the better we resist.

The psalmist said, "I have been young, and now am old; yet I have not seen the righteous forsaken, nor his descendants begging bread" (Psalm 37:25). Although this world we live in is in a rapid downward spiral, we do not have to be governed by circumstances.

Somebody once asked me, "What are you going to do if gasoline reaches $10 a gallon?" My answer: "As long as God has $10 and a penny, we can go." Every time gas or groceries or rent goes up, I make an appointment with my heavenly Father and say, "Father, I need an increase in my finances." I have never been forsaken, and I've never begged for bread. It doesn't matter if bread goes to $19.72 a loaf; God has $19.73!

God's ways are higher than the world's ways—and His ways work. God's knowledge and wisdom supersede the laws by which the world lives. I have never regretted my decision to seek His knowledge and wisdom,

> God's ways are higher than the world's ways— and His ways work.

and to obey His Word—and neither will you. God promises that if we do, we'll spend our days in prosperity and our years in pleasure.

Prosperity Isn't a Get-rich-quick Scheme—It's a Lifestyle

There are actually people who come to our meetings to hear me preach about prosperity that think I'm going to tell them how to get rich quick. Let me be clear: anytime you hear a get-rich-quick message, you'd better run for the door. It's probably illegal.

God doesn't have any get-rich-quick, overnight success, abundance-in-the-next-hour formulas. God's Word deals with a lifestyle. Seeking knowledge and wisdom from God's Word is not something we try for two weeks to see if we get results. We are either committed to living by the Word of God or we're not. Anyone who has one foot in the world and one foot in the Word will never see true prosperity.

God has a plan for His people, and He has a personal and individual plan for each of our lives. Jesus has already paid a tremendous price to ensure God's provision is available to us. It is our responsibility to get our hearts right before God, to be upright in character, and pure in heart.

> Anyone who has one foot in the world and one foot in the Word will never see true prosperity.

Many people believe Jesus was destitute of finances because they read, "Yet for your sakes He became poor, that you through His poverty might become rich" (2 Corinthians 8:9). They also read the Lord's own words, "Foxes have holes and birds of the air have nests, but the Son of Man has nowhere to lay His head" (Matthew 8:20). While it's true Jesus was not born into a family that possessed great worldly wealth, through knowledge and wisdom He obeyed His heavenly Father and thus enjoyed a prosperous life. He said, "The Son can do nothing of Himself, but what He sees the Father do; for whatever He does, the Son also does in like manner" (John 5:19).

Giving to the poor was a part of this manner, or lifestyle. Jesus' disciples knew He had a money box, because when Judas suddenly left the table during the Last Supper, the Bible says, "For some thought, because Judas had the money box, that Jesus had said to him, 'Buy those things we need for the feast,' or that he should give something to the poor" (John 13:29).

When it was time to pay the temple tax, instead of taking the money from the box, Jesus instructed Simon Peter to go to the sea and fish. Jesus said, "Take the fish that comes up first. And when you have opened its mouth, you will find a piece of money; take that and give it to them for Me and you" (Matthew 17:27).

Of course, this wasn't the only time Jesus used the sea to demonstrate knowledge and wisdom in action. We know that, because of the fall, God said man would toil to eat all the days of his life. When Jesus, the living Word of God, told Simon Peter to launch his boat and let down his nets for a catch, the disciple replied, "'Master, we have toiled all night and caught nothing; nevertheless, at Your word I will let down the net.' And when they had done this, they caught a great number of fish, and their net was breaking" (Luke 5:5–6).

My point is, when we make a commitment to a lifestyle of seeking God's knowledge and wisdom, our prosperity is assured—whether or not we have a box full of money or own a fishing business. All we have to do is obey.

God has set forth principles, laws, rules, requirements, and conditions, which if observed and carried out, will result in a life of prosperity and pleasures. However, if these principles, laws, rules, regulations, requirements, and conditions are rejected, the result is bondage. Mankind is God's most prized creation, His crowning achievement. However, man is the only creature created by God that rebels against Him.

> God has set forth principles, laws, rules, requirements, and conditions, which if observed and carried out, will result in a life of prosperity and pleasures.

Donkeys are known for their stubborn nature, yet when the prophet Balaam refused to obey God, it was his donkey who saw the impending disaster and carried Balaam safely away into the field (see Numbers 22). The donkey, being a stubborn animal by nature, had better sense than to disobey God, while the man rebelled against Him.

Birds don't rebel against God. The word of the Lord came to the prophet Elijah during a time of drought saying, "Get away from here and turn eastward, and hide by the Brook Cherith, which flows into the Jordan. And it will be that you shall drink from the brook, and I have commanded the ravens to feed you there" (1 Kings 17:2–4). When God commanded those birds to bring the prophet bread and meat twice a day, the ravens didn't say, "We don't want to. We did it the last time; get the sparrow."

Fish won't disobey God, either. I'm convinced that the moment Jesus told Simon Peter to go to the sea and fish that every fish in the area started hunting for money because none of them knew which would be the first fish caught. They didn't say, "Sorry, God, we don't want to go hunting for money. Simon Peter got himself into this mess, so let him get himself out!" Why didn't they say this? Because God created all things, and all things are subject to His Word.

It was to mankind only that God gave a free will. He wanted His most prized creation to be as close to Him as possible; but He wanted it to be our decision, our choice. We can choose a lifestyle of obedience and prosperity, or we can choose to disobey and suffer the effects of bondage. God has plainly told us that if we obey and serve Him, we shall—not may, or might, or possibly—but *shall* spend our days in prosperity and our years in pleasures. He has also made it abundantly clear that if we do not obey, we shall perish.

So why is it that some people find developing a lifestyle of obedience and prosperity so difficult? If we are totally honest, the answer may sound something like this: "I know what God's Word says about being a blessing to others, but doesn't He understand my resources are limited and it takes all I've got just to make ends meet?" I've said this in times past, when God would speak to me about something He wanted me to do. I would answer, "But, God, you don't understand."

Now isn't that stupid? If anybody understands the intricate details of my life and circumstances, it's God. After all, He's the all-knowing One. There was a time when I faced a problem that looked bigger than anything I'd ever faced before, and I wrongly esteemed the problem as being bigger than God. Suddenly, in my mind, God didn't understand what I was going through.

I remember a time when Carolyn and I were just starting out in our walk of faith. I was still in the National Guard and had just received a call that we were being sent to Fort Polk, Louisiana, for two weeks for special training. This news could not have come at a worse time. I had no money for my family to live on while I would be away. We needed groceries, we needed money for the electric bill, the water bill, and the house note, and to top it all off, my car wasn't running, and I needed money to overhaul the engine.

I had no idea how God could take care of this for me—the need just looked too big. I went into the bedroom to pack my duffle bag and said, "Lord, what am I going to do?" He reminded me of Matthew, chapter six, where He said that He takes care of the sparrows and asked how much better are we than they?

Then He said, "Just trust Me."

I said, "Lord, I trust You, but could You please tell my wife?"

I went into the living room and said, "Carolyn, I don't know how God will do this, but I trust Him."

She said, "Yes, I know. You do what you have to do, and God will take care of the girls and me."

I kissed her and told her how much I loved her, and then, suddenly, there was a knock on my door. I assumed it was my ride, but it turned out to be someone else. The man said, "I'm so glad I caught you before you left. God told me to bring this to you." He handed me a check, turned around, and left. When I looked at the amount, I could hardly contain the joy. The amount of the check was more than enough!

But more than that, the experience taught me nothing is impossible with our God and nothing is too big for Him.

The Bible says Jesus is the express image of God (see Hebrews 1:3). That means Jesus came into this earth and perfectly expressed the will, the nature, the ability, and the ways of God. The Bible says that while Jesus was here, He was "in all points tempted as we are, yet without sin" (Hebrews 4:15). There is no problem or challenge you and I could ever experience that He has not already conquered. He knows what it is like to live on this planet; He knows what it takes for us to please God by prospering in all God has called us to do.

Enjoying the lifestyle of the rich and famous should not be our primary goal in life. Jesus said of His own life, "The Father has not left Me alone, for I always do those things that please Him" (John 8:29). When we choose a lifestyle that is pleasing to God we will be rich, for the Bible promises that "God shall supply all your need according to His riches in glory by Christ Jesus" (Philippians 4:19).

Many people today are considered prosperous from the world's viewpoint, but I don't call a person whose

> God's estimation of a prosperous lifestyle means we not only have enough money to meet our needs and to help others but that we also enjoy peace of mind, physical health, success, favor ... and the list goes on.

stomach is eaten up with cancer prosperous—no matter how much money he may have in the bank. How can anyone be prosperous whose health is ruined, whose family life is in shambles, or whose mind is tormented by doubt, fear, worry, or stress? This is not prosperity.

God's estimation of a prosperous lifestyle means we not only have enough money to meet our needs and to help others but that we also enjoy peace of mind, physical health, success, favor … and the list goes on. This kind of lifestyle only comes through the knowledge and wisdom we find when we spend time in God's Word.

Sadly, however, there are some who turn to God's Word only to see what they can get out of it. I delight myself in the Word of God, not because it will produce something for me, but because it is my Father's personal love letter to me. I don't read it to learn how to acquire things but to learn more about my heavenly Father, to become more like Him, to live a life that is pleasing to Him, and to better serve Him.

> I delight myself in the Word of God, not because it will produce something for me, but because it is my Father's personal love letter to me.

Jesus said, "What will it profit a man if he gains the whole world, and loses his own soul?" (Mark 8:36). Someone said, "I'd rather serve Jesus and be broke than be rich and go to hell." Well, if you establish a lifestyle of prosperity through knowledge and wisdom, you can serve Jesus, miss hell, and still not be broke.

I've been enjoying the benefits of a prosperous lifestyle for more than forty years, and it's worth every minute I've invested into spending time in God's Word. If you've made the decision to establish a prosperous lifestyle through the Word of God, then I have the following three words of wisdom for you.

#1: Separate yourself from the ties of this world.
The apostle Paul said, "Do not be conformed to this world, but be transformed by the renewing of your mind" (Romans 12:2). We have to separate ourselves from the world. We have to get rid of the world's attitude about life and take on God's attitude. In 2 Corinthians 6:17, we read the following: "Come out from among them and be separate, says the Lord." Verse 14 asks, "What fellowship has righteousness with lawlessness? And what communion has light with darkness?"

We can't keep mingling with the world and expect to be blessed of God. We have to untangle ourselves from the world and get rid of our worldly attitudes. We must quit hanging on to what the world has taught us and decide once and for all that we are going God's way.

The Church does not need to be worldly. We should not have the same passions and desires that the world has. I don't have that worldly nature anymore. I am a new creation. My desires have changed. If I catch myself still craving the things that the world craves, that's when I know I need to spend some time with God.

Now, I don't mean that we're not supposed to have the material necessities of life. Jesus didn't say that, either. In fact, He said, "Seek first the kingdom of God and His righteousness, and all these things shall be added to you" (Matthew 6:33). The "things" He was talking about were food, clothing, and shelter—material things.

God wants you to have the material things of life; He doesn't want you living at a standard beneath the world. He wants you to be more prosperous than the world. In fact, He doesn't even want you to be less fashionable than the world. If anything, He wants you to be more fashionable. Where did we ever get the idea that God has no taste, no eye for beauty?

> "Our motivation and life ambition should be to know God more intimately than any other personality in the universe."

When God says we are to separate ourselves from the world, He is not talking about going around in sackcloth and ashes. He is not opposed to our having nice things. What God is opposed to is our following after the lust of this world, having the same ungodly desires the world has.

If our ambition and goal in life is to be rich, then we haven't separated ourselves from the world. Our motivation and life ambition should be to know God more intimately than any other personality in the universe.

#2: Forsake all to follow God.
When God called Abraham to follow Him, He said, "Get out of your country, from your family and from your father's house" (Genesis 12:1). God's promise to Abraham, if he chose to obey, was, "I will

make you a great nation; I will bless you and make your name great; and you shall be a blessing" (v. 2). This promise was connected to a commandment signifying that God required a totally consecrated life. He demanded that Abraham be willing to forsake all to obey Him.

Many people want to obey God, but they want to do so on their own terms. Somebody always wants to play *Let's Make a Deal* with God. It doesn't work that way. You either play by His rules, or you don't play.

You see, God is smarter than you and me. He isn't trying to be hard on us; He knows how to make life work at its best. If we are willing to forsake all and follow Him, He will lead us into an adventurous and exciting life. But there is a price to pay, and not everyone is willing to pay it. God is not trying to take anything away from us. He is not trying to squeeze us into a mold and make us into robots. It is not His intention to deprive us of any good thing. Psalm 84:11 tells us, "No good thing will He withhold from those who walk uprightly." All He wants is our total dedication.

When I was growing up, my greatest ambition in life was to operate my own paint and body shop. I grew up around wrecked cars. My dad was an auto body man with a reputation as one of the best in the state of Louisiana, and he taught me everything he knew. My goal was to be an even better repairman than he was and to one day have my own business. In fact, when I was just a little fellow, my dad and I would talk about it at the breakfast table almost every day.

I'd say, "Dad, one of these days we're going to have our own shop."

Dad would reply, "Yes, when you finish school and get your college education, we're going into business and will have our own shop."

"I can just see it now," I would say. "We'll have a big sign out front that says Savelle and Dad Paint and Body Work."

After Carolyn and I were married, I went to school and worked at different jobs until finally I couldn't stand it anymore. I didn't want to go to college; I wanted to work on cars. So after three and a half years, I quit college and started working on cars.

Then one day my dream came true; I finally got my own shop. I had arrived—or so I thought. I was willing to spend twenty hours a day in that shop to make it go; it had become my god. During that time, I never even thought about the fact that God had called me into the ministry as a result of watching Oral Roberts on television when I was twelve years old. But once I reached early adulthood, I began consistently rebelling against God's call on my life. Now I had my own business, which is all I'd ever wanted, yet I was dying on the inside.

One morning I went to my business, opened the door, and walked through the office and into the tiny restroom just off the shop. I locked the door, sat down on the floor, and cried like a baby. I said, "God, I can't take this anymore. I don't want to live like this; I'm tired of running. I want to do what You want me to do, but I don't know how, I don't know what to say. But I'm giving my life to You, and if You want me to preach, I'll preach."

I made up my mind that day to forsake all and follow

> There is a price to pay when we choose to follow God, but the prosperous life God has already prepared for us is well worth it.

God regardless of what anybody said or thought of me. That's when the Holy Spirit spoke to my heart and said, "Lock yourself away in your guest bedroom for the next three months, give Me no less than eight hours each day, and I'll teach you the Word." I did just that. For at least eight hours a day I prayed, read, studied, and meditated on God's Word, and at the end of those three months, I was on fire to do the work of the Lord even though I didn't have a congregation or an audience to preach to.

I forsook all to obey God, and everything I gave up so that I could serve Him, He's given back to me more than a hundredfold. There is a price to pay when we choose to follow God, but the prosperous life God has already prepared for us is well worth it.

#3: Don't turn back under pressure.
When Abram, whom God later named Abraham, forsook all to follow God, he had no idea what he was about to encounter. "So Abram journeyed, going on still toward the South. Now there was a famine in the land, and Abram went down to Egypt to dwell there, for the famine was severe in the land" (Genesis 12:9–10). Perhaps he thought, "I left my country, and now just look at this mess. I wonder if that was really God talking to me or if it was just something I ate."

We don't know what Abraham was actually thinking, but we do know he persevered to receive the land of promise. "By faith Abraham obeyed when he was called to go out to the place which he would receive as an inheritance. And he went out, not knowing where he was going. By faith he dwelt in the land of promise as in a foreign country, dwelling

> At some point in each of our lives we have to draw a line in the sand and make the decision to run the race God has set before us.

in tents with Isaac and Jacob, the heirs with him of the same promise" (Hebrews 11:8–9).

At some point in each of our lives we have to draw a line in the sand and make the decision to run the race God has set before us. But be forewarned, once that decision is made, it won't be long before we have the opportunity to turn back. Why? Because when God's Word has been sown in our hearts, we become dangerous to God's enemy and ours. Jesus said, "Satan comes immediately and takes away the word that was sown in their hearts" (Mark 4:15).

I've seen many who've stood up and said, "I'm going to live my life God's way from now on." Then, when the enemy comes to steal, kill, and destroy, they begin to weaken. The pressure builds, and they fall apart. Many go back to the world's way of thinking, acting, and living. Oh, they still love God, but because of a lack of commitment and discipline, they end up like the world around them.

The only way Satan can prevent you from living the life God has for you is if you let him. That's why Paul compared a life of commitment to God to an athlete running a race. Once an athlete has made the decision to run in the race, he or she begins the process of training—both physically and mentally. On the day of the race each athlete is assigned a lane, and once the race begins, contenders must follow the set course if they want to complete the race and win the prize.

When the pressure is on, we can draw strength from these words of wisdom and encouragement:

> Let us lay aside every weight, and the sin which so easily ensnares us, and let us run with endurance the race that is set before us, looking unto Jesus, the author and finisher of our faith, who for the joy that was set before Him endured the cross, despising the shame, and has sat down at the right hand of the throne of God.
>
> For consider Him who endured such hostility from sinners against Himself, lest you become weary and discouraged in your souls (Hebrews 12:1–3).

I can tell you from experience, there will be plenty of opportunities to turn back under pressure. But just when it looks like the world has caved in on you, your commitment will really pay off. You'll be able to stand in the midst of adversity and declare, "I am more than a conqueror through Christ, who loves me!"

This has happened to me so many times over the years that this one book couldn't contain all the stories.

However, one comes to mind that I trust will encourage you. It's about a time when I was believing God to purchase a building not too far from our ministry headquarters. We needed the building to house our new Bible school.

When the Holy Spirit pointed this facility out to me, it didn't actually have a For Sale sign on it; but, nevertheless, He told me,

"That's your building." So I had my office manager call and talk to the owners about it. They were actually amazed and said they had been praying about whether to sell it or not, and when we called, they took that as God's leading to do so.

We asked what they wanted for it, and they told us $650,000. It had actually been a small Baptist church, but it was just right for our need. So we agreed on the amount, and we told them we would pay cash for it and would like to close in ninety days.

Now, at that very moment, I did not have an extra $650,000, but I just knew this was our building and that somehow, some way, God would come through for us. He had done it many times before, and I believed He would do it again.

Now, I'd love to be able to tell you that the money all came in the next day, but it didn't. In fact, seventy-five days later, we still didn't have the money. But I wasn't going to back down. I had learned how to persevere, and I had enjoyed the rewards of persevering many times.

It was not until one week before closing that two different individuals came to me and said God had instructed them to contribute toward the purchase of this facility. And what they both gave paid for the building in full. God is faithful.

I'm telling you, it pays to trust God and refuse to give up!

Chapter 3
The Purpose of Prosperity

A number of years ago I had an experience that made a profound impact on my life and ministry where understanding the purpose of prosperity is concerned.

I'd been invited by the pastor of a small church in west Texas to help dedicate the church's new building. During the service, the pastor said he wanted to take an offering for me and for my wife, Carolyn. After the service, when he handed me the envelope, he said, "Now, Brother Jerry, I don't want this to go into your ministry. This is for you and Carolyn personally in appreciation for your work for the Lord and as an expression of our gratitude for what you've done for this church." The offering turned out to be a thousand dollars—a pretty substantial amount at that time.

Normally, all offerings go directly to the ministry. I'm on a set salary, determined by my board of directors, just like everyone else in the organization, and Carolyn and I have to live within our income.

So naturally it was a great joy and blessing to be able to bring in some extra cash just for our own use. In fact, in my mind I already had that money spent on several things we really needed.

But when I got home from that meeting late that night, Carolyn met me at the door and said, "Jerry, there's a couple in town who are being evicted from their house. The movers are setting them and their children and their furniture out on the sidewalk right now. They have no money and no place to move. They don't know what they're going to do. They need a thousand dollars."

"Well, it just so happens that I have a thousand dollars on me," I replied. "When do they need it?"

"Right now!" she said.

By then it was eleven o'clock at night and they needed this money by midnight. We drove to the couple's house where the children were sitting out in the yard watching as their parents were loading furniture into a trailer. They had no idea where they were going. They had no money and no place to even spend the night.

Then the Lord spoke to me and said, "This is the reason I gave you that thousand dollars. This is where I want it to go. That money will keep this family in their home."

And that is just what happened. Because of our willingness to pass on the unexpected blessing God had freely bestowed upon us, that family was able to stay in their home. And God began to bless them and later made them a blessing to our ministry as a result of our giving. They became partners in our outreach, sowing seed into our ministry.

Of all the things I could have bought for myself or for my family with that thousand dollars, nothing could have brought me more happiness than what I received in being the instrument of God to help that family in their time of need.

There is no momentary thrill on earth to compare with the deep, abiding joy of knowing God has so richly blessed us that we can be a blessing to others and prevent a misfortune or catastrophe in their lives. This is the purpose of God's giving to us: to bless us and to make us channels of His blessing to others—including our own families.

The Bible says, "A good man leaves an inheritance to his children's children" (Proverbs 13:22). Clearly, God's idea of prosperity is not for us to have a bare minimum, just enough to meet our own needs. From God's perspective, we are not fully prosperous until we have enough to meet our current needs, plenty to give to meet the needs of others, and then on top of that, enough left over to leave an inheritance for two succeeding generations.

> This is the purpose of God's giving to us: to bless us and to make us channels of His blessing to others—including our own families.

I don't mean to imply that I've reached that level of prosperity yet. I haven't, and not many others have either. But it doesn't mean this level of prosperity is not available to us. We just need to be willing to raise our level of thinking where prosperity is concerned. I believe God wants to raise up some modern-day New Testament Abrahams, people who are blessed and who can be a blessing to all the families of the earth. After all, if the heavyweight boxing champion of the world can go into a ring and earn thirty million dollars in ninety seconds, then surely God can find ways of supplying His children with enough money to bless millions of people around the globe.

I'm not saying we're all going to earn millions of dollars in a matter of minutes. But I believe that more and more of us are going to be blessed and prospered in the days to come because it's part of God's overall plan for the salvation of the world. The Bible says, "The wealth of the sinner is laid up for the just" (Proverbs 13:22 KJV). God is going to transfer some of the wealth of the sinner to some of us, the righteous, so that we have the means to publish the gospel throughout all the world as Jesus commanded us to do.

There are millions of people who have yet to hear the gospel, and you and I are responsible for getting it to them. God wants us to prosper. He wants us to be blessed. Of course, He doesn't want us to allow money to come between us and Him. But at the same time, He doesn't want us to get the mistaken idea that it's impossible to have money and still serve Him. Abraham had riches, and he served the Lord faithfully. So did Isaac. So did many others in the Scripture.

> "There are millions of people who have yet to hear the gospel, and you and I are responsible for getting it to them."

Yes, the Bible does warn us about allowing material goods to interfere with our spirituality. The Bible says that prosperity will destroy a fool (see Proverbs 1:32). But you and I are not supposed to be fools; we are to be wise sons and daughters of God. As children of the King, we ought to have sense enough to know how to handle our heavenly Father's estate.

Fools are destroyed by prosperity. But you and I have access to the knowledge and wisdom of God. We don't have to be foolish with prosperity and thus be destroyed by it. We can use it wisely for God's purposes. Look at what Paul says about God's purpose in prospering us:

> For God, who gives seed to the farmer to plant, and later on, good crops to harvest and eat, will give you more and more seed to plant and will make it grow so that you can give away more and more fruit from your harvest.
>
> Yes, God will give you much so that you can give away much (2 Corinthians 9:10–11 TLB).

At the time of this writing, our television broadcast is aired worldwide via cable, satellite, and the Internet. When God first gave me the assignment to produce a program and air it throughout the world, His plan was staggering. Just the amount of personnel and money that it would take to accomplish the task was mind-boggling. But once I reminded myself that God is El Shaddai—not El Cheapo—I became excited about the possibilities and eager to accept the responsibility He had given me.

I've learned that in order for the Body of Christ to set the stage for the things that are going to happen in this earth before the return of the Lord Jesus, there are a few things in this world we must take hold of—and one of them is television.

The Bible says, "All things were made through Him, and without Him nothing was made that was made" (John 1:3). Television was not made for pornography, murder, prostitution, or any of the diabolical things coming across it now. Television was made for God, and before it's all over, we're going to have greater control of it.

Somebody asked me, "How can you say that? How can the Body of Christ do that?"

I'll tell you how we can do it. The Bible says in Proverbs 13:22 that the wealth of the sinner accumulates and is stored away for the just to receive. Then, at the appointed time, when we are ready, God will put it in our hands. The Bible also says, "The earth will be filled with the knowledge of the glory of the LORD, as the waters cover the sea" (Habakkuk 2:14). How are we going to fill the earth with the knowledge of the glory of God if we don't have the means at our disposal? How are people in the whole earth going to be filled if we Christians don't have the avenue to get that knowledge to them?

The only reason mankind has progressed as far as we have technically, scientifically, mechanically, and electronically is that God is going to use all of this marvelous knowledge and technology for His glory. If God had not had a plan for all these things, man would have been stopped at the creation of the steam engine long ago. The only reason we have been able to achieve what we've achieved is that God has had a plan all along. These marvels were made for Him and for His use (or more precisely, for our use in serving Him).

Did you know that 737s, 747s, and 777s were not made for sinners? Jumbo jets weren't invented for the "jet set" to peddle sin all over the world. They were made for the sake of the gospel. Some people grumble because their pastor drives a nice car. What are they going to do when he owns a 777 and is able to carry a whole congregation into a nation to share the gospel?

You may be thinking, "Dear Lord, our church can't even pay for the new education building, and here this guy is talking about flying to another country in a jet and taking it over for God!" Well, if this idea shakes you, hang around God some more. He's a big, broad, constructive thinker who has no limitations—and neither should we.

Jesus was a messenger of good news, and His message is still going forth. He told His disciples it was profitable for them that He go away (see John 16:7). He said, "Most assuredly, I say to you, he who believes in Me, the works that I do he will do also; and greater works than these he will do, because I go to My Father" (John 14:12).

Jesus was a messenger of good news, but He was limited in how many people He could reach with that good news. Because He was in an earthly body, just as we are, He could only be in one place at a time. If He was preaching in a synagogue in Nazareth, that's the only place people could hear Him. If He was on the shores of Galilee or in the city of Capernaum, a person had to go there to hear the message of good news.

But greater works than those are being done today because Jesus is totally unlimited. He can be in thousands of places at one time because He is not limited to one earthly vessel anymore. He has access to television, the Internet, and modes of transportation that did not exist a century ago. He has the Body of Christ, and all of us are the messengers of good news. As members of the Body of Christ, we have access to all of the kingdom assets that have been prepared for us to use for God's purposes. All that is required of us is that we seek the kingdom.

Things Follow the Seeker

God promised that He would make us "plenteous in goods" (Deuteronomy 28:11 KJV). But this does not mean we are to seek after such things.

Jesus said, "Seek first the kingdom of God and His righteousness, and all these things shall be added to you" (Matthew 6:33). We are not to pursue things any more than we are to pursue prosperity; we don't have to. God's blessings will chase us down and overwhelm us if we will only obey Him (see Deuteronomy 28:2).

I am not seeking or pursuing goods or abundance or prosperity or things. My eyes are on the Creator, not on His creation. I am seeking the kingdom of God and His righteousness, knowing that as I do, all of the things I need to sustain my own life and to accomplish His will in and through me will be added to me as well.

> I am not seeking or pursuing goods or abundance or prosperity or things. My eyes are on the Creator, not on His creation.

Critics of the prosperity message say that we preach and practice the pursuit of prosperity, a seeking after things. If that were true, it would be a terrible indictment. But it's not true. We are not pursuing goods, nor are we teaching others to pursue them. What we are preaching and practicing is the pursuit of God. But we also know and testify to the fact that the Lord has promised to give us abounding prosperity as we seek Him and His righteousness. We expect the Lord to keep His Word. We expect to be blessed, to be made prosperous. We expect to have all of our needs met and to be able to help others as we carry out the Lord's will in this earth.

I want this kind of life. What about you? I'm tired of being the tail; I want to be the head. I'm tired of being on the bottom; I want to be on the top. I'm tired of being the underdog; I want to have the upper hand. And all of this is part of the covenant between our God and us.

I want the kind of life where I'm assured that God not only knows all about my needs but also has made abundant provision for them. He has promised in His Word to see to it that we have plenty for own needs and enough left over to meet the needs of others.

> "Now it shall come to pass, if you diligently obey the voice of the LORD your God, to observe carefully all His commandments which I command you today, that the LORD your God will set you high above all nations of the earth. And all these blessings shall come upon you and overtake you, because you obey the voice of the Lord your God:
>
> "Blessed shall you be in the city, and blessed shall you be in the country.
>
> "Blessed shall be the fruit of your body, the produce of

your ground and the increase of your herds, the increase of your cattle and the offspring of your flocks.

"Blessed shall be your basket and your kneading bowl.

"Blessed shall you be when you come in, and blessed shall you be when you go out.

"The LORD will cause your enemies who rise against you to be defeated before your face; they shall come out against you one way and flee before you seven ways.

"The LORD will command the blessing on you in your storehouses and in all to which you set your hand, and He will bless you in the land which the Lord your God is giving you.

"The LORD will establish you as a holy people to Himself, just as He has sworn to you, if you keep the commandments of the LORD your God and walk in His ways. Then all peoples of the earth shall see that you are called by the name of the LORD, and they shall be afraid of you. And the LORD will grant you plenty of goods, in the fruit of your body, in the increase of your livestock, and in the produce of your ground, in the land of which the LORD swore to your fathers to give you. The LORD will open to you His good treasure, the heavens, to give the rain to your land in its season, and to bless all the work of your hand. You shall lend to many nations, but you shall not borrow. And the LORD will make you the head and not the tail; you shall be above only, and not be beneath, if you heed the commandments of the LORD your God, which I command you today, and are careful to observe them. So you shall not turn aside from any of the words which I command you this day, to the right or the left, to go after other gods to serve them" (Deuteronomy 28:1–14).

Notice verse 11 says, "And the Lord will grant you plenty of goods." The New International Version puts the same verse this way: "The LORD will grant you abundant prosperity." All that is required is that we listen to the voice of God and obey His commandments. In other words, we are to seek His kingdom. He told the children of Israel that if they would do so, all kinds of blessings would come upon them and overtake them, including abundant prosperity.

So, what happens when we experience this abundant prosperity? Not only are our needs met, but we also have enough left over to help others who are in need. Our covenant with God promises that if we obey Him, we will be so blessed, we won't have to borrow from others. Instead, we will lend to many. He promises that if we are obedient to Him, we will be the head, not the tail; we will be above only, not beneath. The Living Bible says, "You shall always have the upper hand" (verse 13).

> Our covenant with God promises that if we obey Him, we will be so blessed, we won't have to borrow from others.

These are the blessings of the covenant God made with

His people, the descendants of Abraham. Do you remember what the apostle Paul said about those of us who are Christians? He said, "If you are Christ's, then you are Abraham's seed, and heirs according to the promise" (Galatians 3:29). What promise is he talking about here? The promise that God will meet our every need—spiritual, physical, and material. We have every right to expect God to grant us abundant prosperity. I am not the one who made this promise, and neither did Paul, nor even Moses; it was God Himself who made the promise.

But that was not the only promise God made to Abraham. When He called the man then known as Abram to leave his country, God said, "I will make you a great nation; I will bless you and make your name great; and you shall be a blessing … And in you all the families of the earth shall be blessed" (Genesis 12:2-3). This is the heritage of the saints: to be blessed and to be a blessing to all families (or nations) of the earth.

Blessed to Be a Blessing

We see that from the time God first conferred blessing upon Abraham, His intent was clear: Abraham would be a blessing to all the families in the earth. This is still how God operates today. In essence, He is saying the same thing to us today that He said to Abraham: "Seek and obey Me, and not only will you be blessed, but you'll also be a blessing to everyone else."

The apostle Paul understood this principle, which he illustrated in his letter to the Corinthians. He wrote, "I realize that I really don't even need to mention this to you, about helping God's people. For I know how eager you are to do it, and I have boasted to the friends in Macedonia that you were ready to send an offering a year ago. In fact, it was this enthusiasm of yours that stirred up many of them to begin helping" (2 Corinthians 9:1–2 TLB).

Paul was saying to the believers in Corinth that he had boasted of them to the Macedonians, emphasizing how eager they were to give help to God's people. He even said it was their enthusiasm that had motivated the Macedonians to make their generous freewill gift. He went on to say, "For God, who gives seed to the farmer to plant, and later on good crops to harvest and eat, will give you more and more seed to plant and will make it grow so that you can give away more and more fruit from your harvest" (2 Corinthians 9:10 TLB).

As we can see, God's covenant with us is twofold. If we are willing to seek and obey Him, He has promised first to bless us personally, and second, to make us to be a blessing to many others. This means that as God's blessings come upon and overtake us, we are then able to pass those blessings on to meet the needs around us. We are not to be selfish with God's blessings; they are given to us so that we can be a blessing to others who are in need.

The expression *to be a blessing* actually means "to be an instrument of God's divine favor." In my book *The Favor of God*, I give the following fourfold definition of favor:

- Something granted out of goodwill
- A gift bestowed as a

> We are not to be selfish with God's blessings; they are given to us so that we can be a blessing to others who are in need.

token of regard, love, or friendliness
- Preferential treatment
- To have an advantage

As I illustrated in the story at the beginning of this chapter about the family who was being put out of their home, it is a blessing to be chosen to administer God's divine favor in the life of another person, preventing misfortune or catastrophe. It is such a joy to recognize how wonderfully God has already blessed us simply by choosing and anointing us to serve as His instruments of blessing to the world.

Unfortunately, many believers do not yet understand this principle. They think they should be blessed of God for their own sake alone, just to meet their own needs. They are only too happy to hear that they will have plenty left over—but for the wrong reason; they think it is to be used to satisfy their own selfish desires. As we have seen, this is not God's plan and purpose in blessing us.

It is both selfish and unscriptural to pray and expect God to provide just enough to meet our own personal needs. It is even more selfish and unscriptural to pray and expect God to provide us wealth and riches to consume upon our own lusts. If you and I are going to be totally unselfish and truly scriptural, we must desire, pray, and expect to receive from God not only enough to meet our own needs but also plenty left over so that we can give joyfully to help somebody else. This is God's plan. This is the covenant.

We've already established that God wants us to live free of bondage because we are the extension of Jesus' ministry in the earth. Jesus had a tremendous reputation as a giver. He didn't come into this world to take; He came to give. Speaking of Himself, Jesus said, "For even the Son of Man did not come to be served, but to serve, and to give His life a ransom for many" (Mark 10:45). Jesus gave His very life for us, and that's exactly what God wants from us—He wants our lives.

God doesn't want just part of you. He doesn't want your money. He wants more than your money. He wants you—all of you. If He can get you, then everything you possess will be available to Him.

Now I want you to realize that God is not saying you cannot have things. God does not want you to go without. Some people have the mistaken idea that God does not want them to have anything. They think that is why He wants them to give all the time. They have interpreted all this to mean that they have to be poor to serve God.

Now, let's rightly divide the Word of God. Whenever God asks you to give, it is first of all because He wants you to receive.

Let's look again at what God said to Abraham: "I will make you a great nation; I will bless you and make your name great; and you shall be a blessing ... And in you all the families of the earth shall be blessed" (Genesis 12:2-3). God said, "I will bless you, and I will make you a blessing." It's one thing to be blessed, but it's something else to be a blessing. If I am blessed, it's because I need to be blessed. If I am a blessing, then I become an instrument of God to help someone else. I become a vessel through which His divine favor flows out into someone else's life.

> Whenever God asks you to give, it is first of all because He wants you to receive.

There is nothing that can compare to being an instrument of God to help someone else be delivered from bondage. I've had more fun being God's instrument to bless someone else. I have learned in my own life just exactly what Jesus meant when He said, "It is more blessed to give than to receive" (Acts 20:35). There is no greater joy in life than to be a blessing. It is a thrill to have something a person needs, to hear God say "Give it to him," and then to see it prevent misfortune in that person's life. There is nothing on earth that can surpass that joy.

God is not asking us to give and to make ourselves available to Him so that we will have nothing. If He asks us to give, then we should give with joy, excitement, and praise. We can do so with confidence once we come to understand that we are blessed to be a blessing.

Chapter 4
Spirit-led Giving Produces the Fruits of Righteousness

In his letter to the Corinthian church, Paul makes reference to something he calls "the fruits of righteousness":

> Now may He who supplies seed to the sower, and bread for food, supply and multiply the seed you have sown and increase the fruits of your righteousness, while you are enriched in everything for all liberality, which causes thanksgiving through us to God. For the administration of this service not only supplies the needs of the saints, but also is abounding through many thanksgivings to God, while, through the proof of this ministry, they glorify God for the obedience of your confession to the gospel of Christ, and for your liberal sharing with them and all men, and by their prayer for you, who long for you because of the exceeding grace of God

in you. Thanks be to God for His indescribable gift (2 Corinthians 9:10–15).

We already know Paul was writing to believers about being a blessing and meeting the needs of others, but what did he mean when he said "the fruits of your righteousness"? As a Jew who had spent years studying the Scripture, he was well acquainted with the writings of the prophet Isaiah, who described the fruit of righteousness like this: "The fruit of that righteousness will be peace; its effect will be quietness and confidence forever" (Isaiah 32:17 NIV). Based on Paul's knowledge of the Scripture, it is probable that his understanding of the fruits of righteousness included the three listed in Isaiah's prophetic word.

Peace is the first fruit. As we become faithful and consistent givers, our lifestyle of giving actually begins to create an atmosphere of peace in us and around us. This is particularly true, and especially important, during times of adversity or when the economy is bad or when things are falling apart. At times like these, people will naturally be drawn to those who manifest the peace of God. This peace will come upon us and overtake us because we are linked to the God of all peace and are living in harmony with Him.

Quietness is the second fruit of righteousness. If ever there has been a time in the history of the Church when people everywhere have needed and hungered for quietness of spirit, it is now. With all the turmoil, harassment, and adversity the Body of Christ is experiencing today, what a wonderful blessing it is to possess quietness of spirit. We can lie down at night, knowing that all of our needs are met. We can do this, not only when things are going well, but at all times, regardless of our outward circumstances.

Confidence is the third fruit mentioned by Isaiah. Although we have needs just like everyone else in the world, we also have something the world does not possess: a sense of confidence—confidence in the Lord and confidence in our own well-being. Despite the problems we may be facing, we are absolutely convinced that God will meet our needs in accordance to His riches in glory by Christ Jesus. This is because we have the God-given assurance that when we are committed to meeting the needs of others, then our own needs will be met by the Lord.

Most of us are familiar with God's promise in Malachi that if we will be faithful with our tithes and offerings, He will open to us the windows of heaven and pour out for us an abundant blessing. The *Lamsa* translation quotes this passage like this: "I will open the windows of heaven for you and pour out blessings for you until you shall say, 'It is enough!'" (Malachi 3:10). I don't know about you, but I haven't yet been so blessed by the Lord that I've had to shout, "Stop, Lord, that's enough!"

In the New International Version, the expression *windows of heaven* is translated as "floodgates of heaven." Can you imagine God literally flooding us with blessings? I know something about what it's like to be flooded.

Some time ago my family and I were the victims of a flash flood in our neighborhood. It was almost unbelievable how hard it rained. The wind was blowing like a hurricane, forcing the rain to fall at such an angle that it came right through the cracks around the windows and doors in our house.

The rainwater was running down the walls and soaking the furniture and carpets. I ran to get a mop, but the water was coming in faster than I could clean it up. I kept trying to sweep and mop up the rising water, but it was no use; I couldn't contain it. Finally I got so tired and frustrated that I just sat down on the floor, in all that water and ruined carpet, and began to laugh. My laughing was the result of my inability to do anything useful.

As I sat there, soaking wet, laughing to myself, I thought of the verse about God blessing in such abundance that it could not be contained. Suddenly the Lord spoke to me and said, "Now this is how I want my blessings to come down upon you."

I got the message. Now I want you to get it—and the blessings that go with it.

I must admit that I don't know many people who have yet been blessed so much that they have had to shout, "It is enough!" But it doesn't mean such blessings are not available to us as Christians. God has said that He will provide a flood of blessings for those of us who will be faithful in our tithing and giving. I believe it's God's will and desire to bless us with just such an overflowing abundance because it's part of His plan for reaching the whole world with the gospel of Jesus Christ.

Giving Is a Lifestyle

When the Lord says in Malachi, "Test me in this ... and see if I will not throw open the floodgates of heaven" (Malachi 3:10 NIV), He is asking us to put Him to the test. And doing so is not meant to be a one-time incident. God's intent is that if we will be continually faithful to Him in our tithing and giving, He will be continually faithful to us in His abundant, overflowing provision for our needs.

What God is asking us to do is to make godly giving a lifestyle—not just an experiment. Many people try this principle of tithing and giving for a few weeks, and then if they don't see immediate results, they decide it doesn't work and they give up. When the overflowing blessing doesn't appear instantly, they quit giving. They don't understand that giving is a lifestyle to be adopted and maintained.

Jesus said this to His disciples, "Greater love has no one than this, than to lay down one's life for his friends" (John 15:13). Now the expression *lay down your life* does not always mean "to die." *To lay down your life for another* means "to put the other person's will, desire, and well-being ahead of your own." To do this, you don't necessarily have to die physically. You simply have to be willing to dedicate your life to working for that person's welfare and benefit rather than for your own. Jesus says this kind of unselfish giving of oneself is the greatest love known to man. It is the lifestyle that He introduced, displayed, and modeled for us, and it is the kind of lifestyle He calls us to adopt.

> What God is asking us to do is to make godly giving a lifestyle—not just an experiment.

Do you remember the rich young ruler who came to Jesus asking what he had to do to inherit eternal life? Jesus told him to go and sell everything he had, give the money to the poor, and then come and follow Him as His disciple (see Mark 10). What was He introducing to that young man? A new lifestyle; a lifestyle of giving.

Jesus didn't tell that young fellow, "I'm sorry, I can't help you because you're rich. You see, you must be poor in order to enter the kingdom of heaven." He did say that anyone who puts their faith and hope into their monetary gains will have a hard time surrendering to the ways of the kingdom of God (see Mark 10:24). But why is that? Because their trust is in their wealth, not in the One who provided the wealth.

Also notice that Jesus did not say it is impossible for the rich to enter the kingdom, only that it is hard. I know many rich people who are having no difficulty at all in serving God. They simply trust in Him instead of in their riches. No matter how rich a person becomes, there are always situations, circumstances, and influences beyond the power of money to control. No one, no matter how wealthy, is immune to the need for the living God.

Jesus taught a lifestyle of giving. Many people, even many Christians, do not understand this simple truth. My purpose in publishing this message is not to tell others how to get rich. If they receive this message and think that what I am preaching is, "All you have to do is give and God will make you rich," they are very much mistaken. I am not talking about getting; I am talking about giving—about an entire lifestyle of giving.

I made the decision long ago that I was going to serve the Lord whether or not I ever got any better off financially. If I never saw a financial miracle, if I never had a better car, if I never got a nicer house, if I never prospered one bit more than where I was that day, I was still going to serve the Lord. Whatever the consequences, I would continue to lay down my life for Him and for the sake of His kingdom and people. Why? Because I was motivated, not by a love for things, but by a consuming love for God and the creatures made in His image.

> I made the decision long ago that I was going to serve the Lord whether or not I ever got any better off financially.

But Jesus has said that those who pursue the ways of the kingdom of God first and His righteousness will be rewarded by the Lord (see Matthew 6:33). All the things they need (not all the things they lust after) will be added to them.

For the past forty-five years I have been seeking the Lord and His kingdom and His righteousness, and for the past forty-five years I have been blessed by Him. I've experienced financial miracles, God has given me nicer cars and a better home than I once had, and I have continued to prosper and be blessed as I've continued to serve Him.

I can't help it if I'm blessed. Everywhere I go, there is a godly blessing just waiting to come on me. Is this so strange, so hard to believe? After all, didn't the Lord promise that if we were faithful, His blessings would pursue us and overtake us? But that isn't the only promise He made to those of us who are godly givers and who obey this commandment to bring all the tithes and offerings into the storehouse. Let's look at some other promises that are ours.

#1: God's blessings will come on us and overtake us.
In the book of Deuteronomy God made this promise to His people: "Now it shall come to pass, if you diligently obey the voice of the LORD your God, to observe carefully all His commandments which I command you today, that the LORD your God will set you high above all nations of the earth. And all these blessings shall come upon you and overtake you, because you obey the voice of the Lord your God" (Deuteronomy 28:1–2).

One day I was out jogging, and as I came upon and passed a man who appeared to be in his eighties, the significance of this passage suddenly struck me. In the same way I'd overtaken that elderly man, so the blessings of the Lord will come upon and overtake us—if we are careful to obey the will and Word of the Lord.

#2: God will rebuke the devourer for our sakes.
As we look again at the words God spoke through the prophet Malachi, we find this additional promise: "And I will rebuke the devourer for your sakes, so that he will not destroy the fruit of your ground, nor shall the vine fail to bear fruit for you in the field" (Malachi 3:11).

Here in this Old Testament passage God assures us that if we will be faithful in our tithes and offerings, He Himself will rebuke the devourer (Satan) for us, for our sakes. We see exactly what this power does for us: it frees us from the power of Satan and protects us against his attempts to steal, kill, and destroy (see John 10:10). After all, "If God is for us, who can be against us?" (Romans 8:31).

#3: God will increase our storehouse of seed.
Turning again to the New Testament and Paul's letter to the Corinthians, we read these words: "For God, who gives seed to the farmer to plant, and later on good crops to harvest and eat, will give you more and more seed to plant and will make it grow so that you can give away more and more fruit from your harvest" (2 Corinthians 9:10 TLB).

Here Paul assures us that if we follow a consistent lifestyle of giving, the Lord will see to it that our storehouse of seed is continually replenished. Why? So that we will have more and more seed to invest into producing more and more fruit. For what purpose? So that we can live in luxury and ease while the rest of the world goes hungry? No! So that we will have more and more fruit to give to meet the needs of others.

Simply put, this is the Christian lifestyle: giving and receiving, being blessed to be a blessing, and experiencing divine prosperity for the sake of all those in need.

Chapter 5
Why God's People Are in Financial Bondage

As members of the Body of Christ, when we sit up at night worrying about our finances and how we are going to feed and clothe our families, it's a clear indication that we've missed something. Something is wrong. Jesus told us to take no thought for these things because our heavenly Father knows we have need of them. He said that if we seek first the kingdom of God and His righteousness, all these things would be added unto us. It isn't right for the Body of Christ to be filled with anxiety, depression, frustration, defeat, and worry. These deadly emotions are a by-product of bondage, specifically financial bondage.

Some men are afraid to face their families at the end of the day because they don't bring home enough to meet the needs. Some families are so tormented by financial bondage that it's destroying their household. And as I said earlier, there are others whose needs are met bountifully, but because they have never allowed God to direct their finances for His purposes, they've never experienced the peace, quietness, and confidence that God has already provided for them. This is yet another form of financial bondage.

If you were to ask someone in financial bondage, "What's your problem?" he or she would likely answer, "My wife …," "My husband …," "My boss …," "My employees …," or "The government …" How many times do you think the answer would be, "Me"? Not very often. And yet, this is exactly where the problem lies. All too often people seek to place the blame on someone else for their financial bondage. We got that from Adam. When God asked Adam why he had disobeyed, his response was, "The woman whom You gave to be with me, she gave me of the tree, and I ate" (Genesis 3:12). Essentially, Adam was blaming both his wife and God for his actions. Ever since that time, people have been pointing their finger at someone else.

Truth be told, if we are experiencing any kind of failure or defeat in our lives, including being trapped in financial bondage, we are the ones who are responsible. If we are not prospering, if we are not successful, the fault is neither with God nor with the Word of God. But we don't have to accept things as they are; we can change them. We just need to recognize the truth of our failure and quit blaming others for it.

> "If we are not prospering, if we are not successful, the fault is neither with God nor with the Word of God."

It is obvious that the world is not obeying God. This is why the world is suffering like it is right now. The world is hurting, governments are failing, economic systems are in chaos, financial institutions are crumbling, and people as a whole are suffering. Just because the world is going the way of financial bondage does not mean the Body of Christ has to follow the trend. We don't have to go down that negative stream. God has said, "My thoughts are not your thoughts, nor are your ways My ways ... For as the heavens are higher than the earth, so are My ways higher than your ways, and My thoughts than your thoughts" (Isaiah 55:8-9).

If we make the decision to go God's way, then we will be on a higher plane than the one on which this world is operating. Even though the world may be headed for ruin, we don't have to go with it. Just because the world is headed for recession or depression or inflation, does not mean we have to go that way.

In chapter 2, we read this scripture: "If they obey and serve Him, they shall spend their days in prosperity, and their years in pleasures. But if they do not obey, they shall perish by the sword, and they shall die without knowledge" (Job 36:11-12). Clearly, obedience to God and His Word is the crucial factor in experiencing the prosperity that has been promised to us. Yet many believers continue to suffer financial bondage. Why is this? I believe there are three major factors that directly hinder us from walking out of financial bondage. They are disobedience, rebellion, and lethargy. Let's examine each one.

#1: Disobedience

God has told us what to do, but we have said His way won't work. He has told us how to do things His way, but we have said, "But Lord, the evening news says ..."

God is telling us one thing; the world is telling us another. We stand in the strategic position of choosing which voice we are going to believe. Many times, because of a lack of commitment to God's way, we lean to the world's way.

Let me ask you a question. Do you have children? If you do, do you require obedience from them? Is it not well with them when they obey, and not so well with them when they don't? The Bible says, "Honour thy father and thy mother ... that it may go well with thee" (Deuteronomy 5:16 KJV). When my kids were young, that's what I told them anytime they were disobedient. I'd say, "It is not well with thee, and it is not going to be well with thee until thou doest right. When thou doest right, it will be well with thee again." If there is one thing my kids grew up knowing, it's this: "It won't be well with thee unless thou obeys thy papa!"

I required obedience from my children. It displeased me when they were disobedient. Now, they were just kids like anybody else's kids. They'd try things here and there, and they'd get corrected and disciplined as needed. We'd sit down together and talk about what's right and wrong. I showed them from God's Word the way they were to behave. Then they'd have the choice to either obey or disobey, knowing that if they disobeyed things would not be well with them. However, if they chose to obey, they would enjoy a life of continuing peace and blessing.

If I had demanded obedience from my children and then disobeyed God myself, I would have been a hypocrite. What kind of an example would that have been for my children? If I expected them to obey me, then they had every right to expect me to obey my heavenly Father, and so does God. If we say to our children, "You are going to obey me or face the consequences," and then turn right around and say to God, "But, Father, You don't understand; I don't want to do that," what kind of example is that?

Anytime things are not going well with me, the first thing I do is check to see if I'm in disobedience in any area of my life. If the Holy Spirit reveals something to me that I'm doing wrong, I quickly repent, ask God to forgive me, and immediately obey what He's told me to do.

There is no place in the life of a believer for disobedience; left unchecked, disobedience leads to rebellion.

#2: Rebellion

You may say, "But I'm not rebelling against God." Well, let's consider what rebellion is.

Take tithing, for example, which is a principle of God. Some people argue about whether tithing is a New Testament teaching and whether New Testament people should be tithers. Those who want to argue against it say that tithing was instituted in the Old Testament under the Law; therefore, as New Testament believers we are exempt from it.

This is not so. Although tithing was part of the Old Testament Levitical law (we find the tithe mentioned as a requirement of the law in the twenty-seventh chapter of Leviticus), this is not the first time tithing is mentioned in the Bible. Tithing goes back to Genesis, the first book of the Old Testament. There we read that Abraham gave Melchizedek, the high priest of God, a tithe of all his possessions to honor God for His goodness of God and all the provisions that He had blessed Abraham with (see Genesis 14:20).

In fact, it appears that it wasn't God who instituted the tithe—it was Abraham. Abraham did not tithe because it was law. The Law hadn't even been given yet. He did it because of his love for God, because of his "attitude of gratitude" for what the Lord had done in his life.

We tithe because we want to. When you realize from God's Word that tithing is a principle in which God expects you personally to take part, your refusal to do so is an act of disobedience. Once you have been told that refusing to tithe is disobedience and you continue to disobey, your disobedience becomes rebellion. The Bible says, "Rebellion is as the sin of witchcraft" (1 Samuel 15:23), and we know God doesn't bless witchcraft!

The reason some believers have not known the kind of prosperity God has made available to us is that there are areas of disobedience in their lives. When we continue to be disobedient, this disobedience leads to rebellion. There is no way God can bless rebellion.

But there is a cure for disobedience and rebellion: it's called repentance. If we will turn to the Lord in sincere repentance, He will forgive us, instruct us, and deliver us from destruction.

There have been times in my own life when God has instructed me by His Word to do something, and as soon as I saw it, I wished I hadn't! I didn't want to hear it, so I tried to ignore it. If I was mad or angry at somebody, I'd try to forget I'd ever read Christ's teachings about strife, disharmony, and the need to forgive. I would find something in the Bible I liked better, something like "bless the Lord, O my soul, and forget not all His benefits" (Psalm 103:2). I liked the part about all His benefits.

You see, we can't ignore God's instruction and expect to receive His benefits. It just doesn't work.

> "If we will turn to the Lord in sincere repentance, He will forgive us, instruct us, and deliver us from destruction."

God is always there with open arms, waiting for the moment we say, "Father, forgive me." When we do, that's when He takes charge. He forgives and cleanses, which puts our sin under the blood of Jesus. He wipes the slate clean and says to us, "Now, start afresh." Then He says, "Go, and sin no more. Don't be rebellious anymore."

Thank God for His grace and for His mercy, but somewhere down the line we should mature enough that we don't constantly need special manifestations of His grace. We should begin to grow up spiritually. We expect our children to grow up. We expect the principles that we lay down to become a part of their nature and their life so that they follow them unconsciously. Take, for instance, getting dressed in the morning.

It is a part of my nature to wear clothes. My mother taught me how to put on my own clothes when I was a little boy. Though I didn't understand why, she made me realize I couldn't leave the house without my clothes on. I don't have to call up my mother every morning and ask her, "Mama, should I put on my clothes today?"

The things we teach our children when they are young will eventually become an integral part of their lives, of their very natures. In the same way, when God instructs us in an area or leads us in a path we are to take, we should do it without hesitancy. We should not even think twice about whether or not we ought to obey.

It amuses me when people come up to me and ask something like, "Brother Jerry, God told me to volunteer in a certain ministry at my church. Do you think I should do it?"

"If God told you to do it, by all means do it!" I say.

Invariably, someone will say, "But you don't understand, I just don't have the time. I work hard all week. Saturday is the day I take care of the house and, if I get the chance, go golfing. By the time Sunday comes around, I'm just too lethargic to move."

Sadly, many believers who would never willingly commit acts of disobedience or rebellion often find themselves bound by lethargy.

#3: Lethargy

Dictionary.com defines *lethargy* as "the quality or state of being drowsy and dull, listless and unenergetic, or indifferent and lazy; apathetic or sluggish inactivity."

Unfortunately, lethargy currently runs rampant in the Body of Christ, with many people getting lazy and slothful where God's call on their lives is concerned. Take, for instance, the local church. In every church there is usually one guy who is full of zeal and who wants to do everything. When the pastor gives him something to do, he gets in there and does it.

When another need arises, the pastor asks for people to get involved, but nobody will. This guy pops up and says, "I'll do it,

Pastor!" So he does it.

Before you know it, he's doing all the jobs. No matter what the need is—teaching a Sunday School class, keeping the nursery, cleaning the restrooms—this guy is right there to do it. Everything gets piled on that one person. Why? Because there is a multitude of Christians out there who are lazy. They say, "If I take that job, I'll be too tied down," "If I get involved in that, I won't be able to do this," or "If I get committed to that, I'll miss the big football game." These people are lethargic where obedience to God is concerned, yet they can't understand why they're having such a struggle all the time.

I'm so glad God doesn't have that same attitude when I'm in need: "I'm sorry, Jerry, but I'm so busy with your wife, Carolyn, I can't help you right now. If I met your needs, I'd be too tired to visit with her."

Aren't you glad God isn't like that? Although I greatly enjoy the company of my wife, I've never run into her at the throne room of God. When I go to God, I never see any of His children there. Every time I'm in need, regardless of the time of day or night, I have God's full attention—and I don't have to stand in line to get it.

That's the way He wants me to be where He's concerned—available. If I make myself available and obedient to Him, then He says I will spend my days in prosperity and my years in pleasures.

There was a young man who worked with our ministry a number of years ago. The first time I met him, I knew he was one of the rare kind who just can't get enough of the Word of God. This young man wanted to work with us, but at the time we didn't have any positions open. He started coming to our church. He took notes on everything that was preached. He studied the Word constantly.

A few months went by, and then one day our office manager said to me, "You know, we need another maintenance man to clean up around here." So I suggested that he check with that young man to see if he was interested.

Most people who come around looking for a job want to start at the top. They want to preach. This young man said, "I'll do anything." When he came on staff, the first thing he did was work outside on the grounds. Whenever I would drive up, he would be out there working. He would have a cassette recorder about eighteen inches long strapped to his side, with headphones on his head and wires running all over his body. He would be playing some of my teaching tapes while he worked.

One day he read in Scripture where God said to bind the Word around your neck and have it on your wrist. He came in the next day with that recorder and headset on as usual, but there was a big band around his arm. He had put some scriptures on that band. Every time he looked at it, he would read it over and confess those scriptures.

Another time, he came to work with a piece of wire wrapped around his neck and sticking out in front of his face. He had some scriptures on it so he could read them while he was hoeing weeds out of the flowerbeds. I had never seen anything like it.

I'm not suggesting that you go to such an extreme. That guy was desperate for the Word, and he didn't care what he looked like or what other people thought or said about him. You see, he had made up his mind that he was going to get the Word, and he didn't care what it took to do it! He just kept obeying God and doing what God said to do. Later he became the pastor of a very successful church. God prospered him.

Lethargy is actually a spirit that comes upon people—a spirit of laziness and slothfulness. It is a tactic of the adversary to get them to lie down, give up, and play dead. Lots of people are affected by this spirit. One reason why lethargy impacts them is the way they were brought up. Some people never had any responsibility, so they don't know how to handle it. Thank God, they can learn.

I was not a disciplined individual before I came to Jesus. In fact, I was very undisciplined. As some folks might say, I was "a compromise going somewhere to happen!" I went through at least ten jobs the first year and a half of my marriage. Why? When things got tough and pressure came, I would just quit. During my first semester at college, I did fine until final exams. I quit school two weeks before the first semester ended. I did not have the principle of discipline built into me as I do now. It was not something I had already developed. But the Word of God made a new man out of me.

Jesus said, "If you abide in My word, you are My disciples indeed" (John 8:31). The word *disciple* comes from the word *discipline*. That's what a disciple is—"a disciplined one." If you continue in the Word, it will discipline you, leaving no room for lethargy. In fact, if you expect to live by God's Word, you will have to become disciplined. It puts a demand on your life.

When you get so desperate for the Word that you will obey God no matter what, then you will spend your days in prosperity and your years in pleasure.

> If you continue in the Word, it will discipline you, leaving no room for lethargy.

Jesus said, "He who has My commandments and keeps them, it is he who loves Me" (John 14:21). If we don't keep His Word, there is every reason to question whether we really love God. It's important to realize these things and make the decision to do whatever we see in God's Word. We must also make the commitment to obey whatever God says to us by the Holy Spirit. We must not be children who are disobedient, rebellious, or lethargic. Rather, we must always be pleasing to our heavenly Father.

God Always Brings His People Out of Bondage

Are you aware that God can see the affliction of His people? God isn't surprised with anything, including the financial bondage suffered by many today in the Body of Christ. Hebrews 4:13 tells us this: "And there is no creature hidden from His sight, but all things are naked and open to the eyes of Him to whom we must give account."

God knows everything about us, even the number of hairs on our heads. He knows everything about His creation, and He can see the affliction and bondage of His people. Hebrews 4:15 says, "We do not have a High Priest who cannot sympathize with our weaknesses." Jesus knows how we feel. He knows the situation we are in. He is a compassionate and merciful High Priest.

Every time God's people, as a whole, have gotten into bondage, the only way they got out of that bondage was through divine intervention.

Why God's People Are in Financial Bondage

Now Moses was tending the flock of Jethro his father-in-law, the priest of Midian. And he led the flock to the back of the desert, and came to Horeb, the mountain of God. And the Angel of the LORD appeared to him in a flame of fire from the midst of a bush. So he looked, and behold, the bush was burning with fire, but the bush was not consumed. Then Moses said, "I will now turn aside and see this great sight, why the bush does not burn."

So when the LORD saw that he turned aside to look, God called to him from the midst of the bush and said, "Moses, Moses!"

And he said, "Here I am."

Then He said, "Do not draw near this place. Take your sandals off your feet, for the place where you stand is holy ground." Moreover He said, "I am the God of your father—the God of Abraham, the God of Isaac, and the God of Jacob." And Moses hid his face, for he was afraid to look upon God.

And the LORD said: "I have surely seen the oppression of My people who are in Egypt, and have heard their cry because of their taskmasters, for I know their sorrows" (Exodus 3:1–7).

In this passage from Exodus we see that God's people were in bondage in Egypt. Egypt was not the will of God for His people. Bondage has never been the will of God for His people. Being dominated by the world and Satan has never been God's will for His people.

God said, "I have surely seen the oppression of my people who are in Egypt [and in our time, in our generation, God has surely seen the financial bondage of His people], and have heard their cry because of their taskmasters, for I know their sorrows" (Exodus 3:7). When you are financially bound, you are full of sorrow. When you can't do what you desire to do, when you can't give the way you want to give, when you stay up all night worrying about how you're going to pay your bills—that's bondage.

There comes a time when our heavenly Father won't put up with a situation any longer. As a parent, you may overlook some mistreatment of your child once, or even twice. But if someone keeps hurting your child, you will intercede in his or her behalf. If your child is being unjustly treated, you won't stand by and allow it to continue.

If we take action in behalf of our children when they are abused, why should it seem so unusual that our heavenly Father would do the same for His kids? Where do you think we got that kind of protective love? We get the similitude of our fatherhood from the Father God. When God's children are being hurt, there comes a time when He cries, "Enough!" At one time in the history of the children of Israel, the people cried out, "God, forgive us. It's our fault that we got into the bondage, but please forgive us!"

The psalmist wrote these words: "Then they cried out to the LORD in their trouble, and He saved them out of their distresses. He sent his word and healed them, and delivered them from their destructions"

(Psalm 107:19–20).

When God's people get fed up with being lorded over by the devil, they will cry unto the Lord, "Father, forgive us for getting into this mess. Forgive us for letting the devil run our lives. Lord, deliver us." Then He will deliver His people out of their bondage.

It was bad news for Pharaoh when God came down on him. He wished he had never heard of El Shaddai. God showed Pharaoh that He is the Most High God.

> When God's children are being hurt, there comes a time when He cries, "Enough!"

Pharaoh thought he could stand up to God, but he quickly learned that he was no match for the Almighty. Neither is Satan! The Bible tells what happened when God began His mighty endeavor to set His people free from Pharaoh's hands:

> "So I have come down to deliver them out of the hand of the Egyptians, and to bring them up from that land to a good and large land, to a land flowing with milk and honey, to the place of the Canaanites ... Now therefore, behold, the cry of the children of Israel has come to Me, and I have also seen the oppression with which the Egyptians oppress them" (Exodus 3:8–9).

God told Moses that He'd come down to deliver His people out of bondage. But how exactly did He do it? He chose a man through whom He could work, saying, "Come now, therefore, and I will send you to Pharaoh that you may bring My people, the children of Israel, out of Egypt" (Exodus 3:10). In his generation, Moses was God's chosen vessel to take the His word of deliverance to His people, and because the people obeyed the voice of the Lord spoken through Moses, they were delivered out of their bondage.

We serve a God who never changes. It is just as much His will for His people to be free from bondage today as it was then. During the 1950s, when people were routinely dying of sickness and disease, God sent a man named Oral Roberts to bring healing to that generation.

Religious-minded men pushed aside the doctrines of the Bible, saying that healing had passed away, that the power of God was no longer in manifestation, that miracles had passed away with the disciples. Despite their unbelief, God told Oral Roberts, "Take healing to your generation." It was not an easy job to stand before the world and say, "God sent me to bring healing to this generation." But, thank God, he did it.

I've always had the greatest respect for Oral Roberts, who was not afraid to stand and preach what God said despite the opposition and antagonism of people. Regardless of the consequences, he kept preaching the message. Today this nation knows about the healing power of God, and Oral Roberts is the man remembered for being directly responsible for this knowledge.

I believed the message Oral Roberts preached, and I walk in divine health today because of his obedience to God's call on his life. I esteem the anointing of God that was on Oral Roberts and also on men like Kenneth Hagin and T. L. Osborn who each made a significant impact on their generation.

I remember a prayer I prayed when I was still new to the ministry. I said, "Lord, give me a greater anointing in my life."

God said, "You're not ready for that yet. You don't know the price it takes for a greater anointing. You're too easily influenced by people."

Then He went on to explain, "For a greater anointing, you have to obey My commands without hesitation. At this point you aren't willing to do that. You are afraid of what people might say if they don't understand your technique."

I wanted to pretend that what God said wasn't so, but you can't play games with God. I knew exactly what He was talking about. The first time somebody said something derogatory about the way God told me to minister healing, my feelings were hurt badly. But through time and experience, I've learned to do what God says to do—the way He says to do it and when He says it ought to be done. When I'm obedient to His instructions, miracles occur. When I'm not obedient, fearing people's reaction or opinion, I fail. It's that simple.

> We must always be more concerned about obedience to God than about public opinion.

We must always be more concerned about obedience to God than about public opinion. Our Lord Jesus was misunderstood, but He didn't care what men thought. Because of His obedience, He was highly anointed.

There was a time I would have resisted writing a book like this because I was too concerned about what people would think or say. But I'm not like that anymore; now I'm only interested in obeying my heavenly Father and delivering His message to my generation.

And the message is this: if you will believe and receive this message, God is going to deliver you from financial bondage.

Part Two
Keys to a Lifestyle of Walking in Prosperity

Chapter 6
Develop a Lifestyle of Obedience

Many years ago while I was in army basic training, I thought, "Dear God, what's a nice guy like me doing in a place like this? What's wrong with these people? Why don't they let me sleep? Why don't they let me eat what I want to? Why do I have to run through these exercises, yelling 'kill, kill, kill' before I can eat breakfast? I don't want to kill anybody; I just want to eat!"

When young men and women join the armed forces of this nation, they are said to be "in the service," which means they are in the service of our nation. We had this saying in the service: "There is the right way, the wrong way, and the army way." We learned to do things the army way, regardless of whether we liked it or not. When you're in the army, you do things the army way. Many times that way seemed absolutely ridiculous to us, but we did it. We learned to develop a lifestyle of obedience.

There comes a time in the life of soldiers in combat when they become grateful for the things they were taught in boot camp. Sooner or later they realize and appreciate the value of obedience to commands, because their very lives depend upon it.

Well, my friend, we are "in the service" of the Lord. And in order to serve Him, we must develop a lifestyle of obedience. We've learned that if we obey and serve Him, our obedience and service will pay off. Some people think about being obedient, but they will not serve. God wants us to do both.

Jesus said, "No one can serve two masters" (Matthew 6:24). There is a responsibility where the Body of Christ is concerned to serve one master, not just give lip service to Him. When we relinquish our relationship with Satan, we become loyal to God. When we say, "Satan, you're no longer the god of my life; I make Jesus the Lord of my life," we've actually committed ourselves to a lifestyle of obedience.

Some people have the mistaken idea that we don't have to commit ourselves to anything; they think we can do whatever we want. Such people never channel their faith toward meeting the needs of humanity and serving God, but that's what faith is all about. That's what faith is for!

God never intended us to develop our faith just so that we could go around accumulating the things we want. God wants our faith strong so that we can be His instrument of blessing to humanity, to stop the ravages of Satan's warfare in the lives of others. If we will get involved in blessing others, God will see to it that all the things we need will be added unto us as well.

Faith has been given to us by God to get His work done, not to serve our own selfish ends. All we have to do is obey His instructions.

Oftentimes people want God to talk to them about daily guidance, but they are not willing to follow the general instructions in His Word. By *general*, I mean the instructions that are for all the Body of Christ. You see, the Bible is for all of us, and I'm expected to live by it just as you are. However, there may be some individual instructions God gives to me personally that He never speaks to you. He may tell me to do something He would never ask you to do. However, we are all required to obey the written Word.

Our obedience to God's Word puts us in a position to have Him speak to us individually by His Spirit to guide us daily in our own personal lives. If we are willing to obey His general instructions, it is likely that we are also willing to obey His specific personal instructions.

Because some people won't obey the general instructions, they have a hard time hearing specific instructions. I hear people complain, "God never talks to me."

I ask them, "Are you obeying the Word?"

"No."

"Then why would God talk to you? If I had written you a letter with instructions about how to live, and you wouldn't read it or obey, I wouldn't bother to try to instruct you verbally."

Some people keep God's Word out on the coffee table so that everybody will be sure to see it when they come in. They may pick it up now and then to read a verse or two at night before they go to sleep. Some may even read it religiously, but they will not obey its contents.

Then they go to God and say, "Lord, please help me. I need some advice."

God asks, "Did you read My Book?"

"Well, no. I don't get anything out of it. I've got to have some help on this situation here. You've just got to tell me how to handle it!"

If this describes you, read the Book! It will give you a general concept of how God operates. From His Word we learn God's thoughts and ways. When we understand His thoughts and ways and are obedient to His general instructions, then we are in a position to receive specific instructions about our specific situations.

Many people want God to help them in their business, yet they won't follow His general instructions about business. They want God to give them specific instructions about their marriage, their health, or their finances, yet they won't obey what He has said in His Word about these things.

We cannot expect to receive help from God if we ignore what He has already told us. We must learn to obey God's Word. There is no other way. When we are willing to obey God's Word (all of it, not just the parts we like), God will have daily communication with us by His Spirit.

Obedience Is Based on the Word of God

Someone asked me one time, "How can you possibly base your life on the Bible when men wrote it and men are capable of making mistakes? How do you know those men were accurate?"

I said, "Well, I just believe that since God is smart enough to create a universe, He is surely capable of getting something across to a man clearly enough for him to get it down on paper the way

He wanted it written."

"Well, I'm just not going to base my life on something men wrote."

"Are you saved?" I asked.

"Yes."

"How did you get that way?"

"John 3:16."

"A man wrote that. It's John 3:16, not God 3:16. A man wrote that."

"Yes, but God inspired it."

"Yes, God inspired it, and I have the audacity to believe it. I'm going to heaven because I believe what John wrote. If I can believe John 3:16, I can also believe 3 John 2 that says, "Beloved, I wish above all things that thou mayest prosper" (KJV). The same man wrote both verses. It was the same man hearing God. If John was accurate in John 3:16, then he was also accurate in 3 John 2."

Someone else asked me, "How can you base prosperity on the Word of God when it was written by mere men? How can you have the audacity to believe circumstances are going to change because of something written by a man?"

I answered, "Because that's what Jesus did."

On the mount of temptation, our Lord Jesus Christ didn't base His victory and success on something God had said to Him in an audible voice. He quoted to Satan something Moses had written, something written by a "mere" man. Jesus said, "Away with you, Satan! For it is written, 'You shall worship the Lord your God, and Him only you shall serve'" (Matthew 4:10). Written by whom? Moses. Not God, but Moses. If Moses had not written the message the way God intended it,

Jesus would have been basing His victory over Satan's temptations on a fallible source. You may be thinking, "What if Moses had missed it?" Well, then his words would have had no effect. They would not have produced enough power to cause the enemy to flee from Jesus. So he didn't miss it, because the power behind what he wrote was evidence that he heard from God.

Peter said that these things were written in times past by holy men who were moved by God (see 2 Peter 1:21). Thank God, we can base our lives on His Word. I know I'm not going to hell because of the words of God's saving grace given through men. God inspired it, breathed upon it, and anointed it. My eternal destiny was changed because of it.

Some people can believe one part of God's Word, yet they have trouble with another part. The reason for this lack of belief is that they haven't developed their faith in that particular area. When we believe all of God's Word is inspired of God and we are willing to obey the principles outlined in it, then our daily communication with Him will become more intimate as He guides us in our affairs.

If you are always willing to do what God tells you, then you are going to prosper. If you hesitate, argue, and try to talk God out of what He's instructed you to do, you will be robbing yourself of prosperity. It's just that simple.

> If you are always willing to do what God tells you, then you are going to prosper.

The Bible says, "The steps of a good man are ordered by the LORD, and He delights in his way" (Psalm 37:23). God wants to order our steps. The word *order* is a military term. To order is to command. God orders, or commands, our steps, but we must be willing to obey. God said through the prophet Isaiah "I am the LORD your God, who teaches you to profit, who leads you by the way you should go" (Isaiah 48:17).

God wants to lead us in the way we should go. If we will obey and serve Him, then we will profit and prosper. If anybody knows how to profit, it's God. If anybody knows how to live well, it's God. I am so thrilled that this all-knowing, all-mighty, and all-successful God was willing to put the principles upon which He lives into a book—the Book. But He didn't stop with His Word. He sent His Holy Spirit—who knows all about how these principles work—to indwell us, to teach us how to profit, and to lead us in the way we should go. All we have to do is be willing to obey and serve.

If I want to arrive at a place of prosperity and success in my life, God already knows the steps necessary to get me there. He has given me His Word and has already laid out the path I should take. He knows what I need to reach every goal or ambition or vision He has placed in my heart. He knows what steps I need to take. If I am willing to let Him order my steps and if I will do exactly what He tells me without hesitation or argument, then prosperity will come to me.

> If I want to arrive at a place of prosperity and success in my life, God already knows the steps necessary to get me there.

An Attitude of Obedience

If I am going to be successful in developing a lifestyle of obedience, the first thing I must do is adopt an attitude of obedience. In his letter to the church at Ephesus, Paul wrote these words: "Children, obey your parents in the Lord, for this is right. 'Honor your father and mother,' which is the first commandment with promise: 'that it may be well with you and you may live long on the earth'" (Ephesians 6:1–3).

God has a family. He is the Father, the head of that family, and we are the children. Surely, anything He would tell children in the natural to do, He would expect from His spiritual children. None of us are born with an attitude of obedience. Until we receive Jesus as our Lord and Savior, taking His nature as our own, we are actually operating in a nature of sin.

I remember how my dad used to try to get through to me when I was a teenager. You see, I was a hot-rodder, always drag racing in the streets, and Dad didn't like it. He would say, "Son, if you don't quit drag racing in the streets, I'm going to take your keys away from you. You're going to tear up your car. You could hurt yourself and endanger the lives of others. I'm not going to put up with it."

He told me all the consequences that could happen if I continued to disobey. He wasn't being mean to me; he just didn't want me to get hurt. He didn't want my life snuffed out because of some foolishness. He knew what he was talking about. At that time, I thought I knew more than Dad. Like all teenagers, I thought I knew it all.

Some of God's kids think they know more than He does. They have the same attitude toward Him as youngsters sometimes have toward their parents. "Oh, what does He know? He doesn't understand." If only we could learn once and for all that God knows what is best for us, then an attitude of obedience would come much easier and quicker. We could save ourselves so much misery if we just operated in an attitude of obedience, but no, sometimes we just have to learn the hard way.

My dad told me why I shouldn't drag race in the street. He told me what would happen if I continued to do so, but I ignored his instructions. At first, my disobedience wasn't deliberate. I would just get tempted to race. I would be fine until somebody pulled up next to me and revved his engine. I really didn't intend to race. I didn't intend to break the law or to disobey Dad, but I couldn't refuse a challenge.

I remember the day I left the rear end of my car lying in the middle of the street and blew up the transmission. When I got home, Dad asked, "What did you do?"

"Drag raced in the street."

"What happened?"

"Tore up my car."

"Didn't I tell you that would happen?"

"Yes, sir."

"Why didn't you obey me?"

"I will now."

Isn't that dumb? But that's what we do. We grow up with an attitude of disobedience, and then we let it carry over into our relationship with our Father God. All God is asking us to do is to obey and serve Him because He knows what is best for us. He led Jesus on His path

> All God is asking us to do is to obey and serve Him because He knows what is best for us.

when He walked on the earth, and Jesus was a total success.

When the apostle Paul gave instructions about the office of bishop, one of the requirements was that the one being considered "must have a well-behaved family, with children who obey quickly and quietly" (1 Timothy 3:4 TLB). This is a perfect description of an attitude of obedience: quickly and quietly. This is the kind of attitude God wants us to have. He wants us to obey Him, not when we get around to it, not when we finally decide that He knows best, not after we've tried everything else, but the moment He says it.

I learned a valuable lesson about obeying quickly and quietly a number of years ago as I was getting ready to go to Memphis for a meeting. While I was packing, God spoke to me about a minister friend of mine and said, "Son, I want you to send Joe some money."

I said, "I'll do that, Lord, just as soon as I get through packing."

I got busy and forgot about what the Lord had instructed me to do. As I was driving toward Memphis, the Spirit of God spoke to me again, "I told you to send Joe that money."

"Lord, I forgot, but I'll do it just as soon as I get to Memphis." I just kept on driving.

I didn't know it at the time, but Joe was believing God for a need he had right then. God wanted to use me to help meet that need, but I was too busy. God and Joe were both doing their part. Joe was praying and believing and the Lord was moving, but I wasn't doing my part.

The sad thing about it was that Joe lived less than twenty miles from my home, but I was going to wait until I had driven all the way to Memphis before I sent him that money. It might have taken a week to get to him.

I got to Memphis and checked into my hotel. As I was lying in bed asleep in the middle of the night, suddenly I woke up. God said, "I told you to send that money to Joe."

"God, I'll do it just as soon as I get back home."

"That's not good enough. Call your wife and tell her to get that money over to him—right now."

"But, Lord, it's the middle of the night."

"He needs it now; in fact, he needed it hours ago. He is standing in faith, believing Me to meet his need. I've talked to several people today about meeting his need and all of them have responded like you." Then He added, "The next time you're in need and your help doesn't come when you need it, don't say a word."

When I heard that, I wanted to get in my car and drive back home right then. Instead, I called Carolyn and said, "Get that money over to Joe. Don't hesitate. God said to do it now!"

Carolyn took the money to him, and he was so grateful because it met an immediate need in his life. Later that day, I called him and told him what had happened and what the Lord had shown me, and it blessed him as much as it did me. When he told me how urgent his need was, I was so glad we didn't just forget about it or say, "Well, it's too late now." That experience turned out to be a valuable lesson I have never forgotten.

God taught me something else in that experience. He said, "Son, there is a spiritual law you released in your life when you acted that way. I said, 'Do unto others as you would have them do unto you' (see Luke 6:31). That's why your needs sometimes go days before they are met. It's not My fault. I spoke, but you caused Me to have to speak to people who delay, who won't obey quickly and quietly, who hesitate and put it off. You set the pattern in your own life because of the way you act. Is that the way you want to live the rest of your Christian life?"

I said, "No, sir, I'm going to correct that. From now on, when You tell me to give, I will do it right away. I'm going to allow You to order my steps and lead me in the way I should go. I'm willing to obey and serve You. Whatever You tell me to do, I'll do without argument, hesitation, or delay."

The attitude in obedience is "quickly and quietly." It does not bring delight or pleasure to you as a parent when your children argue with you about something you've told them to do. Waiting a week before they obey is not pleasing. Neither is it pleasing to God when He says, "Go to the pastor's house and give him a day off; clean his house for him." But we answer, "If I do that, who's going to clean mine? Besides, I didn't like what he preached last week." If you act that way, you will rob yourself of that day's prosperity.

> "The attitude in obedience is "quickly and quietly.""

Peter learned about the connection between obedience and prosperity when he had an attitude change following an all-night fishing expedition. As Jesus was preaching one day to a crowd of people who had gathered to hear Him, He saw Simon Peter bringing his boat ashore and asked if He could stand in the boat and preach from it. Simon Peter agreed, and when Jesus had finished His sermon, He turned to Simon Peter and said, "Launch out into the deep and let down your nets for a catch" (Luke 5:4).

Simon Peter replied, "Master, we have toiled all night and caught nothing; nevertheless at Your word I will let down the net" (Luke 5:5). After a night of unsuccessful fishing, Simon Peter was probably ready to wash his nets and then go home and rest. But as a result of his obedience, he caught so many fish in his net that he had to call his partners to bring another boat to help him.

This is how Jesus wants us to respond to His instructions too. When He instructs us to do this or that, to go here or there, to give something, or to make ourselves available for a particular work, He wants us to answer, "Yes, Lord, at Your word I will do it."

When we develop a lifestyle of obedience, God will lead us in the way we should go, and everything we set our hand to will prosper.

Chapter 7
Develop a Lifestyle of Faith

If we are going to walk in the level of prosperity God has prepared for us so that He might use us to touch the lives of others, we must develop a lifestyle of faith. As Christians, we have a heritage of faith; it is our birthright as the seed of Abraham, who is commonly known as "the father of faith."

The fourth chapter of Romans describes Abraham as "the father of all those who believe" (Romans 4:11). Verse 3 tells us that "Abraham believed God, and it was accounted to him for righteousness." Because God knew Abraham would believe Him and be obedient, God chose him to be the man through whom He would establish His covenant of blessing for His people, and indeed for all people who would accept His covenant by faith. In this covenant, which means "contract, or agreement," God promised that if Abraham would obey and serve Him, God would abundantly bless not only him but his seed as well: "And in you and in your seed all the families of the earth shall be blessed" (Genesis 28:14).

Romans 4:13 tells us, "The promise that he would be the heir of the world was not [given] to Abraham or to his seed through the law, but through the righteousness of faith." In other words, God promised that Abraham and his seed would inherit the world. That promise did not come because of the Law, which came some 430 years later; it came because of Abraham's faith in God. Galatians 3:29 assures us that "if we are Christ's, then we are Abraham's seed, and heirs according to the promise." This means everything God promised Abraham belongs to us. We are Abraham's seed, and the blessings of Abraham are ours.

The Bible declares in both the Old and New Testaments that the just shall live by faith (see Habakkuk 2:4, Galatians 3:11). If we are going to live in accordance with the way God has ordained, then we need to understand certain things about faith. We need to understand how to live it and how to fully consecrate our lives to God so that there will be no hindrance to His blessings coming upon us. We want them to come on us just as they did upon Abraham.

> We are Abraham's seed, and the blessings of Abraham are ours.

Because Abraham believed God by faith, God referred to him as His friend (see Isaiah 41:8). I would like to be called the friend of God. I would like to be so intimate with God that He would not do anything without first revealing it to me. That's the way it was with Abraham. God had such an intimate relationship with Abraham that He would not destroy Sodom and Gomorrah until He had first talked it over with His friend (see Genesis 18:16–33). In fact, it was Abraham who dictated the conditions for that destruction. Now that is intimacy with God.

We have the ability to walk that closely with God. To do it, we need to know something about how Abraham got into that favored position. We need to know what he did to be able to enter into that kind of blessing and prosperity, how he entered into that life of faith. Let's look again at the fourth chapter of Romans where the apostle Paul is describing Abraham's life, using him as an example of the life of faith:

> And he received the sign of circumcision, a seal of the righteousness of the faith which he had while still uncircumcised, that he might be the father of all those who believe, though they are uncircumcised, that righteousness might be imputed to them also, and the father of circumcision to those who not only are of the circumcision, but who also walk in the steps of the faith which our father Abraham had while still uncircumcised (Romans 4:11–12).

Notice the phrase "who also walk in the steps of the faith which our father Abraham had." God is instructing us New Testament believers to walk in the steps of our father Abraham, the father of faith.

Living by Faith

To some people, living by faith means "quit thy job." I'm here to say that it does not. Living by faith does not mean you should quit your job. In fact, if you're going to quit your job, then you had better know how to live by faith first, or you will starve.

Some people believe the life of faith is a life of laziness. Jesus lived by faith, and He said, "My Father worketh hitherto, and I work" (John 5:17 KJV). In another place He said, "I must work the works of Him who sent Me" (John 9:4). Jesus was sent into this world by the Father to work, and He told us, "As the Father has sent Me, I also send you" (John 20:21).

When you live by faith, you will never work so hard or enjoy life more. I don't work less now that I live by faith. I work more, and I enjoy it more.

We are to walk in the steps of the faith of our father Abraham. What was it about Abraham that caused God to bless, honor, and esteem him so much? His faith, of course. As we look at the eleventh chapter of Hebrews—the greatest faith chapter in the entire Bible—we can pinpoint what it was about Abraham's faith that God liked: "By faith Abraham obeyed when he was called to go out to the place which he would receive as an inheritance. And he went out, not knowing where he was going" (Hebrews 11:8). Abraham was willing to follow God, even though He could not see the end result of his obedience.

Some people will tell you that whatever it is you are trying to do can't be done. Did you know that, according to the laws of aerodynamics, it is impossible for the bumblebee to fly? His body is too big for his wings, which makes it scientifically impossible for him to get off the ground. The only problem is, the bumblebee doesn't know this. You see, bumblebees don't read scientific journals. They don't listen to what the scientists say, and if they did, they wouldn't believe it. The bumblebee believes he can fly, so he zooms right over the heads of those learned men of science who stand earthbound and shout up at him, "Come back down here. It's impossible for you to do what you're doing!"

That's what I like about being a believer. While the world stands around saying, "It can't be done," we just keep on flying. That's what the life of faith is all about.

Abraham was called of God to go into a place he knew nothing about. He had no evidence in the natural that such a place even existed. God just told him to get up and leave, so he did. And as a result of Abraham's faith and obedience, he enjoyed the land of promise with Isaac and Jacob, who also received and carried on this promise from God (see Hebrews 11:8–9).

Some people seem to think that living by faith is a life of being insecure, but that's not the truth. I'm not stumbling. As a matter of fact, I'm even more secure and confident. The Bible says, "The steps of a good man are ordered by the LORD, and He delights in his way. Though he fall, he shall not be utterly cast down; for the LORD upholds him with His hand" (Psalm 37:23–24). I'm not walking insecurely, and I'm not walking in darkness. On the contrary, I am living in the light and security that faith in Christ Jesus produces.

The people walking in darkness are those who find their security in the world's system and way of thinking—people who don't know my God. Yes, I walked in darkness before I met God, before I had developed this relationship with Him. But, now I walk in the light, I don't walk in uncertainty. Like the apostle Paul, I'm confident, I walk by faith and not by sight, I know in whom I have believed, and I am fully persuaded that He is able to perform that which He has promised (see Philippians 1:6, 2 Corinthians 5:7).

Somebody said, "But those people who live by faith never know what's going to happen."

Yes, we do. I know what's going to happen in every area of my life. When I'm believing God and standing on His Word, then the fulfillment of His Word is going to happen. I don't know exactly how God will do it, and I learned long ago to quit trying to figure it out. That's not my responsibility. My responsibility is to walk in obedience to Him, to follow what He says, and to believe He is able to perform His Word. God's responsibility is to confirm His Word with signs following. How He does it is His business. When I walk in the light of God's Word, I'm not walking in uncertainty.

Abraham was a man who obeyed God, and the Bible says great blessings came upon him. God promised Abraham that if he would walk in the light of His Word and do all that he was commanded, He would bless him and his seed abundantly. Abraham entered into that covenant with God. He walked in the blessings of the Old Covenant. Thank God, we are Abraham's seed. We are heirs according to the promise, and we have a right to live in those blessings.

When Jesus gave Himself at Calvary, He did not do away with the blessings of Abraham—He enlarged upon them. They are still ours today. God promised to bless Abraham, and the Bible tells us "after Abraham had patiently endured, he obtained the promise" (Hebrews 6:15).

To develop a lifestyle of faith and obtain all God has promised us, there are three things we need to understand about living by faith. First, faith is not need-minded; second, faith is seed-minded; and third, faith always sees needs as opportunities to prosper. Let's examine each of these three characteristics of a lifestyle of faith.

#1: Faith is not need-minded.
Some time ago I was scheduled to fly to Tulsa to speak at a meeting. Before I left home, I tried to talk to the Lord about some critical needs in my life and ministry. Instead of answering the way I had expected, He told me, "When you get to Tulsa, I want you to give away your van." I dropped the subject.

On the plane, I again approached the Lord about my pressing situation. "Father, I really need to talk to You about my needs. It just seems they have become overwhelming."

Again the Lord spoke to me and said, "When you get to Tulsa, I want you to give away your van." So again I dropped the subject.

A while later, during a quiet moment, I took up my case with the Lord for the third time. "Father, during this meeting in Tulsa I'm going to have a little time between services, and I really need to talk to You about my needs."

Once again came His response: "When you get to Tulsa, I want you to give away your van." But this time He went on. "Also, there are five preachers in Tulsa who have become discouraged and are about to give up the ministry. I want you to give each of them a suit of clothes." So once more I decided not to continue the discussion.

Finally, when I just couldn't hold back any longer, I declared to the Lord, "Father, I've just got to talk to You! You know we've completed our international headquarters in Fort Worth and have just moved into them, but there are still lots of things we need. More land, for instance, and more buildings. But we don't have the money to get what we need, and …"

"When you get to Tulsa, I want you to give away your van and five suits of clothes."

It was then that it finally hit me what was happening. Every time I tried to talk to God about my need, He talked to me about seed. Now, that wasn't deep. As children of God, all of us should understand this principle because we are seed-planting people. But, if you are like me, you have probably noticed that as you have moved forward in the call of God that your needs have grown larger and larger. If this is the case, then you are probably wondering where in the world the money is going to come from to meet those steadily increasing obligations. It's okay to wonder, but when we become so focused on our needs that they are all we think about, we have become "need-minded." When we become need-minded, we have hindered our own ability to walk in faith—and we know faith is not need-minded.

If you and I are going to walk in the prosperity God has already provided for us and learn to deal successfully with the issues of life on God's level, then we cannot be need-minded. We must instead learn to operate the way God operates by thinking and acting as our heavenly Father thinks and acts. That's why every time I tried to talk to Him about my needs, He spoke instead about planting a seed. I've learned that the Lord only discusses solutions, not problems.

Our Father is well aware that the needs of the Body of Christ are growing at a tremendous rate every year. I've never had so many needs in my whole life as I have been experiencing the past year or so. Our ministry is growing and reaching out more now than ever before. Obviously, the more we grow, the more needs we produce. Every time my faith grows, my needs grow right along with it.

The same is true of you. Every time your faith reaches a new and higher dimension,

> I've learned that the Lord only discusses solutions, not problems.

so does the need that faith venture produces. What it took to keep you going last year is not nearly enough to keep you afloat this year. Why? Because your needs increase as your faith, your ministry, and your sphere of influence grow and expand. This is just natural in the life of a believer. The danger in all of this otherwise healthy growth and expansion is that if we are not careful, we will become need-minded.

This is what I believe the devil is trying to do to the Body of Christ today: make us need-minded. He doesn't place new needs upon us; they come as a natural result of our growth, expansion, and outreach. The deeper we penetrate into enemy territory, the more resistance we meet from our enemy and the greater our need for larger amounts of supplies. So our adversary, the devil, seeing that he can't stop our advance, sets out to cause us problems. He begins throwing up obstacles in our path, setting traps, laying ambushes, snipping away at us from all sides, doing his best to disrupt our vital supply lines.

In short, Satan is going all out to pressure us into taking our mind off our objectives and goals, to focus instead on our problems.

In our Christian battle, you and I must not become need-minded. Doing so will cause us to give into pressure and become discouraged. If we keep our attention and our eyes trained on our seemingly insurmountable needs, we'll be tempted to give up the fight and quit. That's exactly what the enemy wants us to do.

There is a way out of this situation: His name is Jesus.

Did you know our Lord had needs when He walked this earth giving His life in ministry to others? One time, when He was preparing to enter Jerusalem, He sent two of His disciples ahead into the city. He told them that in a certain place they would find a young colt no man had ever ridden. They were to untie the colt and bring it back to Him. If anybody asked what they were doing taking the animal, they were to answer, "The Lord hath need of him" (see Mark 11:1–3).

So we see from this statement that Jesus did have needs. But was His mind centered on His needs? Does God in heaven spend His time pondering and worrying over the needs of His children, His Church, or the world? The answer to both questions is *no*.

What has the Lord said to us about our needs? Has He told us to just grin and bear it until we all get to heaven where we won't have any more needs? Or has He indicated that there is an answer to our needs, here and now?

I remember when Brother Kenneth Copeland first came to my hometown and began preaching the message of faith that was to revolutionize my life. The message was brand new to me then; I had never heard anything like it. But I believed it, and I wanted to know more about it.

Some time later, I was talking with Brother Copeland and I told him, "I believe your message, and I'm doing all I know to do to put it into practice in my life. I understand how some things work in the kingdom of God. I understand how healing comes, but there is one thing I don't understand: I just don't know how to talk God into meeting my needs."

I will never forget what Brother Copeland told me that day. He said, "Jerry, God has already done all He is going to do about your needs."

I sat there and pondered what he'd said for a minute. Then I answered, "You're kidding. He's not going to just leave me in this mess. Is He?"

That was not what he meant. He wasn't saying that God was not going to do anything about my situation. What he meant was that God had already made provision to meet my every need.

Jesus does not have to hang on the cross and die over and over again every time somebody needs to get saved. God has already met the need for salvation for all mankind, once and forever. He is just waiting for each individual person to receive by faith what He has already provided by grace.

The same is true of all our physical and material needs. God has already made provision for our salvation or deliverance from poverty, lack, and want, just as He has already made provision for our salvation from sin and death. This provision was paid for by the death, burial, resurrection, and ascension of our Lord and Savior, Jesus Christ, who now sits at the right hand of the throne of God where He lives and continually makes intercession for us (see Hebrews 7:25). The actual terms of this provision were spelled out long ago in the Old Testament.

> "God has already made provision for our salvation or deliverance from poverty, lack, and want, just as He has already made provision for our salvation from sin and death."

"But that's the Old Covenant," some say. "What about the New Covenant?"

In the New Testament Jesus said, "Your Father knows the things you have need of before you ask Him" (Matthew 6:8). Later on God spoke through the apostle Paul, assuring us that He will provide for our every need through the endless abundance of His riches by way of Jesus, our Savior (see Philippians 4:19).

When we go before the Lord about our needs, we are not springing something on Him that He is not aware of. He already knows what our needs are before we ask. What the Lord showed me in all this is the fact that when we spend hours and hours in prayer, day after day, going into great detail about our every need, we are wasting His time and ours.

So if that is not the way we are to go to the Lord about our needs, how should we approach Him? Hebrews 4:16 gives us the answer: "Let us therefore come boldly to the throne of grace, that we may obtain mercy and find grace to help in time of need."

What is God telling us? He is saying, "Dearly beloved, I know all about your need before you come to Me. I have promised to supply all your need according to My riches in glory by Christ Jesus. Don't fret, worry, or fear; just come to Me and freely receive all that I have given you in Christ."

We can see God's attitude about our needs. To come before Him and spend hours discussing our needs is to put the emphasis on the wrong thing. That's just what I was doing that day on my way to Tulsa: I was focusing on my needs—that is, until the Lord made one statement that put the whole subject into perspective for me. He said, "Son, if you are going to walk in the kind of prosperity it takes to meet the needs of the ministry I've called you to, you have to stop being 'need-minded' and instead become 'seed-minded.'"

You see, God is not need-minded like we are. I kept telling God about my need, and He kept talking to me about my seed. I wanted to focus on what I did not have; God wanted to focus on what I did have. That's the way God works.

#2: Faith is seed-minded.

Can you imagine being blessed so abundantly, being so prosperous, so plenteous in goods, that your entire wage or salary could be used as seed to be invested in the lives of others?

The point I am making is that God is not need-minded; He is seed-minded. When God had needs of His own, He fulfilled those needs by giving. He needed the redemption of mankind; He needed a family. So what did He do? He planted a seed: He gave Jesus.

Our Lord told us plainly that "unless a grain of wheat falls into the ground and dies, it remains alone; but if it dies, it produces much grain" (John 12:24). God sowed His seed, His only Son, Jesus, into the earth and reaped in return a harvest of sons and daughters. He planted the best seed heaven had to offer; He did not plant worthless seed. No, He chose and planted the very best He had. And He reaped the best of all harvests, human souls. The Lord got that family He wanted—you and me.

Our seed-minded God has made provision for the meeting of every last one of our needs. He invites us to come boldly to His throne of grace to obtain mercy and to find grace in our time of need.

> God sowed His seed, His only Son, Jesus, into the earth and reaped in return a harvest of sons and daughters.

Now I want to tell you what God in His grace accomplished through the seed-minded churches in Macedonia: "Though they have been going through much trouble and hard times, they have mixed their wonderful joy with their deep poverty, and the result has been an overflow of giving to others" (2 Corinthians 8:2 TLB). They were experiencing hard times and poverty, but when God poured out His joy upon them, the result was an overflow of giving (or seed planting) to others.

It is time for us to become leaders in the spirit of cheerful seed planting. Now, this is a virtue I have had to learn gradually over a long period of time. When I first started out in the ministry, I was not blessed with the understanding of this principle. I was working for Kenneth Copeland, and we had traveled to minister at a meeting. I'll never forget the first time he asked me to come to his room and pray with him. That was way back in 1972. After two or three days of gathering for times of intense prayer, Brother Copeland announced, "The Lord has told me that in order for us to launch into this television ministry, I am to give away my airplane."

Now, since I remembered that we had flown to that meeting in that very same plane, my first question was, "How are we going to get home?" That was real seed-mindedness on my part! You can see what level I was operating on. All I could think about was our need. But I soon learned better.

As if giving away an airplane wasn't enough, Brother Copeland went a step further. He announced that since the engines had a lot of flight time on them, he was going to have them repaired before he gave the airplane away.

I thought to myself, "That's crazy. Let the man you give it to do that." For the life of me I couldn't figure out why anyone would spend several thousand dollars to repair a plane he was about to give away. Then I discovered the reasoning behind the action.

Brother Copeland explained, "The reason I want to put this plane in first class condition is that by giving it away, I am planting a seed, and I don't want to reap a worn-out plane in return."

When most of us are called upon to give away some of our possessions such as clothing, we usually go through our closets and pick out everything we don't like—whatever is worn, out of style, uncomfortable, unbecoming, or just plain ugly. What a sacrifice! When we do this, do you know what we are going to get in return for each old cast off garment we give? An abundant return of exactly the same thing. Why? Because every seed produces after its own kind (see Genesis 1).

If you and I are to be leaders in seed planting, we must give the way God gives: we must give the best. Then the best will come back to us in multiplied form. That's what happened to the church in Macedonia, to whom Paul wrote these words: "I am not giving you an order; I am not saying you must do it, but others are eager for it. This is one way to prove that your love is real, that it goes beyond mere words. You know how full of love and kindness our Lord Jesus was; though he was so very rich, yet to help you he became so very poor, so that by being poor he could make you rich" (2 Corinthians 8:8–9 TLB). Those Macedonian believers were greatly enriched because of the love they showed in their giving.

In the hard times in which you and I are now living, people need a good example. In these days when there are so many ministries failing, so many churches cutting back or shutting down, so many believers becoming discouraged, being sidetracked, and dropping out, there are multitudes begging for someone to stand up and provide them an example and a model. That example and model should be us, the seed-minded saints of God who are the leaders in cheerful giving.

> "If you and I are to be leaders in seed planting, we must give the way God gives: we must give the best."

#3: Faith always sees needs as opportunities to prosper.
Although a lifestyle of faith is a lifestyle of seed-mindedness, we are still going to have needs. But a seed-minded believer always sees those needs as opportunities to prosper.

I love the Old Testament story of Elijah the Tishbite who, along with the inhabitants of Gilead, was experiencing a season of drought and famine:

> Then the word of the LORD came to him, saying, "Get away from here and turn eastward, and hide by the Brook Cherith, which flows into the Jordan. And it will be that you shall drink from the brook, and I have commanded the ravens to feed you there."
>
> And it happened after a while that the brook dried up, because there had been no rain in the land.
>
> Then the word of the LORD came to him, saying, "Arise, go to Zarephath, which belongs to Sidon, and dwell there. See, I have commanded a widow there to provide for you" (1 Kings 17:2–4, 7–9).

Notice what the Lord said to the prophet in both instances: "I have commanded the ravens to feed you; I have commanded a widow to provide for you." Past tense. The Lord had already made provision for Elijah before He sent him on his way:

> So he arose and went to Zarephath. And when he came to

the gate of the city, indeed a widow was there gathering sticks. And he called to her and said, "Please bring me a little water in a cup, that I may drink." And as she was going to get it, he called to her and said, "Please bring me a morsel of bread in your hand."

So she said, "As the LORD your God lives, I do not have bread, only a handful of flour in a bin, and a little oil in a jar; and see, I am gathering a couple of sticks that I may go in and prepare it for myself and my son, that we may eat it, and die."

And Elijah said to her, "Do not fear; go and do as you have said, but make me a small cake from it first, and bring it to me; and afterward make some for yourself and your son. For thus says the LORD God of Israel: 'The bin of flour shall not be used up, nor shall the jar of oil run dry, until the day the LORD sends rain on the earth'" (1 Kings 17:10–14).

This woman had already been instructed to take care of the prophet. When he arrived, he asked her to feed him, but she was not seed-minded. She was need-minded. She was focused on the facts of the moment, which were that she had only a few provisions that she and her son planned to eat before they died.

What she didn't realize was that within the opportunity to give, or plant a seed, God was also giving this widow the opportunity to increase her own income. He wanted to meet both her immediate and her future needs, but because she was so need-minded, she couldn't recognize the wonderful opportunity being offered to her.

Every one of us has needs. Great needs. Pressing needs. And the Lord has many opportunities for us to give so that we can have those needs met. But if we are like this poor need-minded widow who could not recognize an opportunity to prosper, we will never reap the abundant harvest God has already prepared for us.

The prophet instructed the woman to feed him first, promising her that if she would do so, then her provisions of meal and oil would not run out until the day of famine was over. The Bible says, "So she went away and did according to the word of Elijah; and she and he and her household ate for many days. The bin of flour was not used up, nor did the jar of oil run dry, according to the word of the LORD which He spoke by Elijah" (1 Kings 17:15–16).

I believe God is giving each of us an opportunity right now to prepare ourselves for what lies ahead down the road. He is commanding us to keep planting seeds, assuring us that if we do, our resources will not fail during the hard times to come. He is telling us walk in faith and to become seed-minded rather than need-minded. When we do, we'll begin to see our needs as nothing more than opportunities to prosper.

After all, developing a lifestyle of faith is an essential key to living a life of prosperity.

Chapter 8
Develop a Lifestyle of Giving

Many people, whether they are in financial bondage or they are just not operating at the level of prosperity promised in God's Word, make the common mistake of thinking they need some major change in their circumstances. Some believe the answer is to get a new job or move to a different part of the country or just win the lottery.

But God has a better solution, a permanent solution. God wants us to develop a lifestyle of giving, of sowing seed. Let's look at the instructions He gave to Isaac during a time of famine:

> There was a famine in the land, besides the first famine that was in the days of Abraham.
>
> Then the LORD appeared to [Isaac] and said: "Do not go down to Egypt; live in the land of which I shall tell you. Dwell in this land, and I will be with you and bless you; for to you and your descendants I give all

these lands, and I will perform the oath which I swore to Abraham your father."

Then Isaac sowed in that land, and reaped in the same year a hundredfold; and the LORD blessed him. The man began to prosper, and continued prospering until he became very prosperous (Genesis 26:1–3, 12–13).

Here we see that while many others were seeking refuge from the famine by fleeing to Egypt, Isaac was instructed by the Lord to stay in the land and sow. The result of his obedience was a hundredfold return on what he sowed.

Giving is God's solution to financial famine. Not to withhold, but to give, to sow in time of adversity. Once again we see that God is seed-minded, not need-minded. I believe that developing a lifestyle of giving is key to coming out of a financial crisis.

Do you remember the incident that took place at the table during the Last Supper? Jesus knew Judas was making plans to betray Him, and during the meal He turned to Judas and said, "What you are about to do, do quickly" (John 13:27 NIV). The disciples heard this exchange between the two, but thought since Judas kept the moneybag, Jesus was instructing him to go and give money to someone in need. Obviously, Jesus had a reputation for giving.

This is the kind of reputation the Lord wants you and me to have as His children. He has promised that as we remain in the land (in Him and in His Word and will) and are faithful and obedient to continue to sow in time of famine, He will provide for us a multiplied return, a bountiful blessing.

I want to share a favorite scripture found in Proverbs: "There is one who scatters, yet increases more; and there is one who withholds more than is right, but it leads to poverty. The generous soul will be made rich, and he who waters will also be watered himself" (Proverbs 11:24–25).

This passage assures us that it is possible to give away and yet grow richer. The world doesn't understand this principle. They say it is impossible. However, Jesus said, "The things which are impossible with men are possible with God" (Luke 18:27). The world says to get all you can and then hold on to it. God says just the opposite; He says to develop a lifestyle of giving.

The New International Version says, "A generous person will prosper; whoever refreshes others will be refreshed" (Proverbs 11:25 NIV). Now this concept of refreshing was not thought up by a few preachers who go around the country preaching prosperity. Modern-day man didn't write these words; they were written centuries ago under the inspiration of the Holy Spirit. This is not my plan and promise; it is God's plan and promise.

> The world says to get all you can and then hold on to it. God says just the opposite; He says to develop a lifestyle of giving.

The concept is simple: God has decreed that the person who refreshes others through a lifestyle of giving will be similarly refreshed. In other words, it is possible to give freely yet gain even more. Giving always refreshes, and those who refresh others with material goods will themselves be refreshed by the Lord.

If you will refresh others, God will see to it that you are refreshed. If your attitude is "nobody ever gives me anything," then you should know why this is true in your life. It's that you don't give anything to anybody else. You are reaping what you sow.

Some people tell me, "Well, when I need money, I don't give, I just work, work, work."

I believe Christians ought to work. God believes that too. In fact, work was His idea. The Bible clearly teaches this spiritual principle. Paul went so far as to say, "But if anyone does not provide for his own, and especially for those of his household, he has denied the faith and is worse than an unbeliever" (1 Timothy 5:8).

In 2 Thessalonians 3:10, he writes, "For even when we were with you, we commanded you this: If anyone will not work, neither shall he eat."

Finally, in 1 Thessalonians 4:11–12 of the New International Version, Paul reminds readers, "Make it your ambition to lead a quiet life: You should mind your own business and work with your hands, just as we told you, so that your daily life may win the respect of outsiders and so that you will not be dependent on anybody."

The Bible indicates the reason we should work is so that we will not be dependent on others and that we will have seed to sow in the lives of those in need. As Christians, you and I do not work for a living; we work for a giving.

If you will keep on giving, faithfully and consistently refreshing others, the Lord will see to it that you are refreshed in return. In the book of Ecclesiastes we find this familiar poetic metaphor about giving:

> Cast your bread upon the waters,
> For you will find it after many days.
> Give a serving to seven, and also to eight,
> For you do not know what evil will be on the earth.
>
> If the clouds are full of rain,
> They empty themselves upon the earth;
> And if a tree falls to the south or the north,
> In the place where the tree falls, there it shall lie.
> He who observes the wind will not sow,
> And he who regards the clouds will not reap.
>
> As you do not know what is the way of the wind,
> Or how the bones grow in the womb of her who is with child,
> So you do not know the works of God who makes everything.
> In the morning sow your seed,
> And in the evening do not withhold your hand;
> For you do not know which will prosper,
> Either this or that,
> Or whether both alike will be good (Ecclesiastes 11:1–6).

This passage of scripture is so important to a full and clear understanding of godly giving that I would like for us to read it again, this time in The Living Bible translation:

> Give generously, for your gifts will return to you later. Divide your gifts among many, for in the days ahead you yourself may need much help.
>
> When the clouds are heavy, the rains come down; when a tree falls, whether south or north, the die is cast, for there it lies. If you wait for perfect conditions, you will never get anything done. God's ways are as mysterious as the pathway of the wind and as the manner in which a human spirit is infused into the little body of a baby while it is yet in its mother's womb. Keep on sowing your seed, for you never know which will grow—perhaps it all will (Ecclesiastes 11:1–6 TLB).

In this passage we see a vital principle of godly giving: give generously, for your gifts will return to you later. Some people may say, "I just don't believe that." Well, whether you believe this principle or not does not change the truth of it. But what you believe affects whether or not it works for you.

There was a little slogan that used to appear on bumper stickers: "God said it. I believe it. That settles it!" The truth is, if God said it, it is already settled, whether you or I or anybody else believes it or not. Nevertheless, our believing it is to our advantage.

God's Mysterious Ways

You might be thinking, "I just don't understand how I can give away something and expect God to give it back to me."

I know you don't understand this concept; neither do I. That's what The Living Bible means in Ecclesiastes 11:5 when it says, "God's ways are as mysterious as the pathway of the wind and as the manner in which a human spirit is infused into the little body of a baby while it is yet in its mother's womb." Of course, we don't understand how such things happen; we just know they do.

It is not necessary that we fully understand God's principles to benefit from them. We must simply learn them, believe them, and act upon them.

For example, we don't know how seeds bring forth plants or fruit. We just know they do, so we sow seeds into the ground, patiently tend and nurture them, and then reap an abundant harvest. That's what God expects us to do with the good seed of His Word.

I don't understand how the Lord can use me to plant a seed gift in the ministry of another man of God and then provide me in return a generous gift from someone else who lives in California—someone I don't even know!

> It is not necessary that we fully understand God's principles to benefit from them. We must simply learn them, believe them, and act upon them.

For instance, early in my ministry I was in a church in Illinois for a series of meetings. I preached seven sermons without receiving a single offering for my ministry because the Lord spoke to me and told me not to accept an offering.

"You know, Father," I pointed out to Him, "I do have a budget to meet."

But still, I was obedient. I did as I was told to do; I preached all week long without receiving an offering. After the meetings were over, I left town.

On my way back home to Texas, I stopped to speak at a Full Gospel Businessmen's banquet. As I began to prepare for the service, the Lord again spoke to me and said, "Don't take an offering here either." So I didn't.

The next morning I began the long drive back home. After a while, I exited the freeway to have lunch, walked into a nearby restaurant, and looked for a place to sit down. Now I didn't walk in carrying a huge Bible or wearing a sign proclaiming that I was Jerry Savelle, "the, great man of God." I wasn't even wearing a suit and tie. I had on comfortable traveling clothes like everyone else there.

I want you to realize that this incident happened at a time when not too many people had even heard of me. But after I sat down and ordered my meal, an elderly couple got up from their table, came over, and politely tapped me on the shoulder.

"You don't know us, but we know who you are," they told me. "We were sitting over there talking about you before you came, and we looked up and there you were."

Then the lady told me, "I said to my husband, 'Why, that's Jerry Savelle right there! Isn't it?' And he said, 'You know, I believe it is.'"

They went on to tell me that before I had entered the restaurant, the Lord had spoken to them about giving me an offering. They had already decided to mail it to me at my office in Fort Worth as soon as they got back home. But when they got up to leave, they saw me walk in. The Lord immediately instructed them to give the offering to me in person, right then and there. That generous offering was more than enough to cover the expenses of the Illinois meeting.

I don't know how that sort of thing happens, I just know it does, time and time again. Understanding how it happens is not my responsibility. My responsibility is to plant the seed. It is God's responsibility to meet the need.

The Bible tells us only that our godly gifts will come back to us; it doesn't say how or when. I wish I could explain how a gift is returned in multiplied form or when it will happen, but I can't. However, I do know one thing: the time between sowing and reaping is the most important and exciting time in our lives. It is a time that becomes a great adventure in faith. The secret is to sow faithfully, generously, and regularly so that we can expect a continual flow of godly gifts in return.

> My responsibility is to plant the seed. It is God's responsibility to meet the need.

Looking again at our passage of scripture from the book of Ecclesiastes, we see that the Bible says, "Divide your gifts among many, for in the days ahead you yourself may need much help" (Ecclesiastes 11:2 TLB).

What is God saying to us? He is trying to prepare us for the future, for whatever may be coming down the road. If things are tough now, if we are having a hard time making it through these days, then how will we ever be able to face even worse times to come?

From all indications, world conditions are not going to improve in the future; they are going to continue to worsen. But that doesn't mean the Body of Christ has to be overcome by the world and its failing economic and social order. Just because the world's system is failing, there is no reason that the Church of Jesus Christ must go under. If anything, the failure of the world's system should herald the greatest resurgence and revival of the Church in the history of mankind.

I believe what God really desires is, when the world is at its worst, the Church be at its best. The world's darkest hour will be the Church's brightest hour. That is what the prophet Isaiah was referring to when he told the people of his day,

> Arise, shine;
> For your light has come!
> And the glory of the LORD is risen upon you.
>
> For behold, the darkness shall cover the earth,
> And deep darkness the people;
> But the LORD will arise over you,
> And His glory will be seen upon you.
> The Gentiles shall come to your light,
> And kings to the brightness of your rising (Isaiah 60:1–3).

The days ahead will not be our brightest hour if we do not develop a lifestyle of giving. Without sowing into God's kingdom and into the lives of others, we will end up as dark as the world. The Lord has instructed us to divide our gifts—to sow them—among many so that we will have much help in the days to come.

You may have planted and sowed, day in and day out, for weeks or even months with no apparent results. Don't get discouraged. How do you know that today is not the appointed day of harvest? How do you know that the next seed you sow is not the very one that will cause all the other seeds to come to fruition? Divide your seed among many, and then expect to harvest a manifold return on your sowing.

Some time ago, I was talking to the international director of our ministry in Africa. We were discussing the battle we had gone through in that land. At every step we'd had to combat corruption and opposition. But God had told us to go into that area and pull down the strongholds of Satan, and that was exactly what we had done, troubles or no troubles.

Our loyal workers had lived under constant threat, in turmoil and stress twenty-four hours a day, with never a moment to relax. They had not been able to let down their guard for an instant. The warfare they had engaged in had been not only spiritual but also natural. In fact, some people there had been so opposed to the ministry, they had actually hired assassins to kill members of our staff.

But despite the dangers, obstacles, and opposition from both man and Satan, we had kept on planting seeds into that outreach, week after week, month after month. My director said that, after nine long months of seeming failure, we had finally begun to see a return on our investment in those precious African lives.

He told me that now he and his staff could hardly contain their joy because every new day brought a new victory over the forces of evil and darkness. All the seed we had faithfully and consistently planted had suddenly begun to grow and produce fruit for the kingdom of God.

The principle of this story? Let's not be like the man who heard God rewards the tither, so he began to tithe faithfully—but when he didn't see any return on his tithes within three weeks, he concluded tithing didn't work and stopped giving. This man expected to harvest as soon as he had planted, so he gave up too soon and ended up losing everything he had sown. Let's not make that mistake. Let's keep planting those seeds, because the Bible promises that "in due season we shall reap if we do not lose heart" (Galatians 6:9).

Remember that God's ways are not man's ways; in this sense, they are mysterious.

Seven Benefits of a Lifestyle of Giving

Just as our obedience to God and His Word produces blessing in our lives, developing a lifestyle of giving comes with its own benefits. I have identified seven of these benefits based on the familiar words God spoke through the prophet Malachi:

> "Bring all the tithes into the storehouse, that there may be food in My house, and try Me now in this," says the LORD of hosts, "if I will not open for you the windows

of heaven and pour out for you such blessing that there will not be room enough to receive it" (Malachi 3:10).

Let's look at these seven benefits one at a time.

#1: Giving releases our faith in the faithfulness of God.
Did you know that giving is an act of faith? When we give of our material means, especially what we need to live on, it releases our faith in God and in His absolute faithfulness. If we didn't believe that God is faithful to His Word, which promises to reward us richly for our giving, then we would be tempted to withhold our gifts for our own use.

Perhaps this is why so many Christians hold back from giving freely; they are afraid of losing what they give away, what they think they need so desperately. They have no real faith that God will keep His Word and meet their every need in accordance with His riches in glory as He promised (see Philippians 4:19).

#2: Giving establishes God's covenant in our lives.
The covenant God made with Abraham in the Old Testament also applies to us today. We have seen that, because of Abraham's faith, God promised to bless him and make him to be a blessing to all the families of the earth. These blessings also were pronounced upon the seed (or the offspring) of Abraham forever. We saw that, because of what Jesus Christ has done for us, we are now the seed of Abraham and have been restored to our rightful position as sons and daughters of

God. As such, we are heirs to the promises God made to Abraham—heirs to the covenant.

The way you and I establish (or ratify) the covenant in our own individual lives is by acting upon the provisions of it. Through our faithful and obedient giving in response to God's command, we activate the provisions of that covenant, which guarantees that we will be blessed with the same blessing God poured out upon our spiritual ancestor Abraham. The covenant worked for Abraham in his day, and it will work for us in our time.

#3: Giving links us to the highest authority in the universe.
God promised that when we give our tithes and offerings to Him and His work, He will open the windows of heaven and pour us out such an abundant blessing that we won't be able to contain it. Notice who does the pouring out: it is God Himself. We don't have to look to others to meet our needs even though God may use people in that role. Rather, it will be God who undertakes to bless us and to make us to become a blessing to many others.

Our giving puts us into contact and covenant with the Supreme Power of the Universe, who cannot and will not fail.

#4: Giving releases the power of God in our behalf.
As we have said, God promised that when we tithe, He will do something for us in return. One of the things He does is to open the windows of heaven and pour us out a blessing in abundance.

The New International Version translates the promise like

this: "'Bring the whole tithe into the storehouse, that there may be food in my house. Test me in this,' says the LORD Almighty, 'and see if I will not throw open the floodgates of heaven and pour out so much blessing that there will not be room enough to store it'" (Malachi 3:10).

It is clear that, by our giving, the power of God is released in our behalf. Our giving literally opens to us the floodgates of heaven.

#5: Giving enlarges our capacity to receive from God.
As we continue to give, we continue to increase in our ability to receive. The more we give, the greater our return; the greater our return, the larger our tithe; the larger our tithe, the larger our return. Our capacity to receive from God just keeps growing and growing, in an ever-increasing cycle of giving, receiving, and blessing—for ourselves and for many others.

Many years ago I heard Oral Roberts say that he had long ago gotten out of the realm of obligation and into the realm of faith. He said that the tithe is not a debt we owe, but a seed we sow. I like the biblical concept "freely we have received, so freely we give."

The best part of this concept is that it doesn't end there. The more freely we give, the more freely we receive. But the opposite is also true: the more freely we receive, the more freely we give—"not grudgingly or of necessity [out of obligation]; for God loves a cheerful giver" (2 Corinthians 9:7).

Can you imagine the impact we could make on this world if we enlarged our capacity to receive from God? We would ultimately be able to finance the greatest revival in the history of the Church.

#6: *Giving increases our capacity to receive more of God.*
Our giving reveals that we not only want more *from* God but also more *of* God in our lives. In the book of Acts, we read a story about a Roman army officer named Cornelius, described as a godly man of prayer, who gave generously to charity. The Bible describes an experience Cornelius had:

> While wide awake one afternoon he had a vision—it was about three o'clock—and in this vision he saw an angel of God coming toward him.
> "Cornelius!" the angel said.
> Cornelius stared at him in terror. "What do you want, sir?" he asked the angel.
> And the angel replied, "Your prayers and charities have not gone unnoticed by God" (Acts 10:3–4 TLB).

We know that God prizes cheerful givers, and because Cornelius was such a cheerful giver, his giving did not go unnoticed by the Lord. And what was the result of his giving? Cornelius and his whole household received the Holy Spirit. They were the first Gentiles to be granted the salvation of the Lord.

This tells me that my giving, like that of Cornelius', enlarges my capacity to receive not only more *from* God but more *of* God. But more than that, it also shows we are willing to take something that belongs to us and invest it freely into God's kingdom. As a result, God increases our capacity to receive more *from* Him and *much* more *of* Himself.

#7: Giving increases the fruits of our righteousness.
As we learned in chapter 4, peace, quietness, and confidence are the fruits of righteousness that are increased by our giving. In other words, when we give to the Lord and His work, He guarantees us freedom from fear, anxiety, worry, stress, unrest, and loss of sleep. Instead, we live in peace and confidence—in quiet dwelling places.

We still don't know how or when our promised return will be manifested, but we know it will be. We wait on the Lord in quietness of spirit and confidence of heart because we know that He who has promised is faithful (see Hebrews 11:11).

Moving from a place of financial bondage into the freedom of prosperity God has already provided for us requires us to make His Word the final authority in our lives. We can enjoy all the benefits of a prosperous life if we are willing to apply the principles set forth in God's Word and develop a lifestyle of giving.

Chapter 9
Develop a Lifestyle of Pursuing God

Without a lifestyle of total dedication to the pursuit of God, we may experience temporary prosperity, but it will not be real or permanent.

Pursuing riches will only hinder us from enjoying real Bible prosperity. I want to give an example of a man who stopped pursuing God and tell what happened to him as a result. His name was Uzziah, the king of Judah. The Bible unfolds the story of King Uzziah in Chronicles 26:

> Now he went out and made war against the Philistines, and broke down the wall of Gath, the wall of Jabneh, and the wall of Ashdod; and he built cities around Ashdod and among the Philistines. God helped him against the Philistines, against the Arabians who lived in Gur Baal, and against the Meunites.
>
> Also he built towers in the desert. He dug many wells,

for he had much livestock, both in the lowlands and in the plains; he also had farmers and vinedressers in the mountains and in Carmel, for he loved the soil.

Moreover Uzziah had an army of fighting men who went out to war by companies, according to the number on their roll as prepared by Jeiel the scribe and Maaseiah the officer, under the hand of Hananiah, one of the king's captains. The total number of chief officers of the mighty men of valor was two thousand six hundred.

Then Uzziah prepared for them, for the entire army, shields, spears, helmets, body armor, bows, and slings to cast stones. And he made devices in Jerusalem, invented by skillful men, to be on the towers and the corners, to shoot arrows and large stones. So his fame spread far and wide, for he was marvelously helped till he became strong.

But when he was strong his heart was lifted up, to his destruction, for he transgressed against the Lord his God (2 Chronicles 26:6–7, 10–12, 14–16).

We see that not only was Uzziah prosperous but also he was very strong because he was "marvelously helped" by the Lord. He received honor and glory; his name was spread abroad. Yet in reading the rest of the story, we see that Uzziah turned from trusting in God to trusting in his own strength and his own riches, and he ended up in a sad condition.

In the eighth chapter of Deuteronomy, God warned the children of Israel that when they had settled in the Promised Land and were prospering, they were to remember the Lord their God, for it was He who had given them power to get wealth. Uzziah did not do that. As a result, he was stricken with leprosy and cut off from his throne and his family, and he died in shame and agony (see 2 Chronicles 26:21). How different this story would have been had Uzziah only changed his attitude and returned to God instead of riches.

It isn't hard to change your attitude and lifestyle. Second Timothy 2:21 tells us, "If anyone cleanses himself from [sins], he will be a vessel for honor, sanctified and useful for the Master, prepared for every good work." All we have to do is spend time in God's Word, pursue Him, and fellowship with Him. He will cleanse us from the effects of sin, making us vessels of honor that He can work through to bless others. When we develop a lifestyle of pursuing God, He knows we can be trusted with His riches. This is what happened to a man named Jacob, whose name was later changed to Israel after he began his pursuit of God.

Jacob's entire story is found in chapters 25 through 33 of the book of Genesis. As the grandson—and thus the seed—of Abraham, Jacob was already entitled to blessings. However, he had an older brother named Esau. As the eldest son, Esau had a birthright, which meant he was entitled to special blessings reserved for the firstborn. Jacob knew this, and he desired to be rich. He had seen the prosperity of his grandfather Abraham, and he wanted to be like him.

The only problem was that Jacob didn't want to do what his grandfather had done to receive that prosperity. He didn't want to consecrate his life to God. Jacob put riches and prosperity above

God. He sought them first. Because of his lust for wealth, he would do anything to obtain riches.

Jacob bargained his brother, Esau, out of his birthright and deceived his father, Isaac, into bestowing Esau's blessing upon him. As a result of his deception and his cunning ways, Jacob was forced to flee from his enraged brother. He had to leave home, never to see his mother again. (Seeking the wrong thing will always get you into trouble.)

Later Jacob settled down in a certain area of the country. There he saw a woman he desired. Her name was Rachel. Her father said Jacob could have her in marriage in exchange for seven years of labor. So Jacob worked the next seven years for Rachel's father. When the time was up and the veiled bride was presented to Jacob, it was Rachel's sister Leah, not Rachel, that he got. Jacob's father-in-law had tricked him into working seven long years for a woman he didn't want. Then he had to agree to work seven more years for Rachel.

While Jacob was working those fourteen years for his father-in-law, his wages were cut back ten times. Jacob was learning a hard lesson about deception: deceive, and thou shalt be deceived! He had to pay dearly for the trickery he had practiced against his father and his brother. You see, dishonesty won't work; impurity of heart won't work. Deception has a way of falling back on the head of the one who practices it. Jacob had wanted riches, but he ended up working for a man who deceived him and reduced his wages continually.

It was not until Jacob had an encounter with the Lord and wrestled with an angel that he began to prosper. The only reason he was wrestling with an angel was that he was fleeing for his life. He had heard that his brother, Esau, and a company of four hundred men were out to kill him. As the events turned, Jacob was forced to experience hard times as a result of his deceptive attitude. He had to learn commitment the hard way.

After he met the angel and wrestled with him, Jacob became a new man. He was changed. To mark that transformation, God gave him a new name. The name *Jacob* means "deceiver," so God called him *Israel*, which means "the prince of God."

Jacob had an experience with God. It was not until he had put God first place in his life and began to pursue Him, as his grandfather Abraham had so faithfully done, that Jacob became a prosperous man.

Later in his life when he was returning to his own country laden down with possessions, he said to his brother Esau, "Please, take my blessing that is brought to you, because God has dealt graciously with me, and because I have enough" (Genesis 33:11).

Jacob had made a vow unto God, and God blessed him. God increased Jacob's substance and prospered him. What kind of vow did Jacob make to be so blessed by God? He said, "If God will be with me, and keep me in this way that I am going, and give me bread to eat and clothing to put on, so that I come back to my father's house in peace, then the Lord shall be my God … and of all that You give me I will surely give a tenth to You" (Genesis 28:20–22).

Can you see the key to prosperity here? It's total dedication to God. Pursue God, not riches. The apostle Paul warns the Body of Christ against pursuing wealth and riches and putting them before God:

> But those who desire to be rich fall into temptation and a snare, and into many foolish and harmful lusts which drown men in destruction and perdition. For the love of money is a root of all kinds of evil, for which some have strayed from the faith in their greediness, and pierced themselves through with many sorrows.
>
> But you, O man of God, flee these things and pursue righteousness, godliness, faith, love, patience, gentleness (1 Timothy 6:9–11).

We see clearly that those who seek after riches have erred from the faith and will pierce themselves through with many sorrows. We are not to follow their example. We are to learn from it and save ourselves from having to experience their unhappy fate by keeping our hearts pure, by following after righteousness, and by allowing the fruit of the Holy Spirit to operate through us.

A Relationship of Trust

If we want God to trust us with His riches, then we have to trust Him with ours. If we want God to bless our business, then we have to be about our Father's business.

It stirs me to put my trust in God. It stirs me to keep Him first place, to keep my heart pure, and to keep myself in a position where He can always trust me. As long as He can trust me, I'll never go without. My God promises that by His Son, Jesus Christ, He will graciously provide for me every necessity, and more, from His unlimited storehouse of wealth in glory (see Philippians 4:19).

How I wish that those who criticize the message of divine prosperity could realize, once and for all, that God's prosperity is not a get-rich-quick scheme. Getting rich isn't God's message, and it isn't my message. Principles like the hundredfold return are not set up by God to be used to fulfill the lust for things. Too many of God's people are violating God's laws, trying to make this work for them in a way that God never intended. If we don't do it God's way, it won't work. God is not seeking a greedy, selfish, get-all-we-can people; He is seeking a peculiar people, a royal people, a people who have set their minds on pursuing Him and not on things.

> If we want God to trust us with His riches, then we have to trust Him with ours. If we want God to bless our business, then we have to be about our Father's business.

Jesus never implied that those who follow Him are to live in poverty and lack. He didn't require that lifestyle of any who followed Him when He walked this earth in the flesh. It was not His intention that the disciples live as paupers. He was careful to point out to them that anyone who had given up anything to follow after Him would receive that thing back a hundred times over (see Matthew 19:29).

Why weren't the disciples immediately rich? Because they didn't learn everything overnight. Peter had a hard time getting the principles taught by Jesus straight, and I'm sure the others did too. Even Abraham didn't learn everything in one night. Abraham was brought up in a home where his father was an idol worshiper. That's one reason God told him to leave his family and his father's house: He wanted Abram to learn to trust Him.

The more God can trust a person, the more that person is going to be blessed. That's the way it works. We have to give trust if we expect to be trusted. At times God has told me, "I can trust you with a greater anointing and with more finances now." At other times I have had to prove I was ready for more.

The day I launched out into my own ministry, I wasn't preaching before crowds of five thousand to fifteen thousand people as I regularly do now. I wasn't immediately made responsible for millions of dollars. I couldn't have handled it. That's why some preachers get into trouble. God begins to advance them, they begin to progress, and then they get their eyes off God and onto things. They stop pursuing God and, instead, start to depend on riches. I've learned from others' mistakes. I've watched what has happened to some people and learned how to avoid those pitfalls.

I didn't enter the ministry to get rich. I'm not preaching for wealth. I'm preaching because I have compassion for humanity. I am a messenger of God, and I want people to know they don't have to live in bondage. Anything I get as a result of being obedient to God will be His doing, not mine.

You see, I know my heart, and that's the key. You need to search your heart and find out what your motives are. If you have a pure heart and are sincere before God, you will prosper because God can trust you.

Some people have been suppressed financially for a period of years; however, in that suppression, they have proven themselves honest before God. God will not let such folks remain suppressed. Then, there are others who have had all they wanted of this world's goods. They have been selfish and greedy with their possessions. They will find themselves becoming abased, being brought down. Why? Because it's established in God's Word: "Whoever exalts himself will be humbled, and he who humbles himself will be exalted" (Matthew 23:12).

> If you have a pure heart and are sincere before God, you will prosper because God can trust you.

The rich young ruler had this kind of wrong attitude toward things. His trust had turned from God to his riches. He could not let go of them to follow Jesus. He had become a slave to his wealth, which really constitutes idolatry. Money can become an idol—a god—to people. You see, God is the Most High God. The Bible says He is a jealous God (see Exodus 20:5). He will not allow Himself to be shared with any other god. He will not accept a divided heart from His people.

When Jesus instructed this man to dispose of his possessions, He didn't intend for him to remain poor after he'd given everything away. In fact, for that man to have remained poor after obeying Jesus' commands would have violated the laws of God. The Bible says, "He who has pity on the poor lends to the LORD; and He will pay back what he has given" (Proverbs 19:17). That young man would have gotten it all back again because it is the law of God. God said, "My covenant I will not break, nor alter the word that has gone out of My lips" (Psalm 89:34).

Jesus wanted that man to put his trust in God, not in riches. Evidently his trust in riches was so strong that the only way to break it was to have him give it all away. Jesus knew what it would take for this man to put his trust back in God. He required that he sell what he had, give the money to the poor, and follow Him.

Please do not misunderstand the point of this story. Jesus is not asking us to stay broke. He is asking us to leave all and serve Him. If we do this, He won't allow us to remain in need. For Him to do so would violate God's law.

Jesus was offering this man the greatest financial venture (and adventure) of his entire life. If he had done what Jesus commanded and put his trust in God and not in his riches, God would have seen to it that he got back exactly what he had given away (many times over) and that he had great possessions. All of it, and more, would have come back to him. But this fellow was shortsighted. All he could see was what he had right in front of him. He blew the best deal he could ever have been offered.

Perhaps you've done the same thing. It's regrettable, but it's not unalterable. It can be changed. The moment you prove to God that your trust is in Him and not in your possessions—the moment you demonstrate that your heart is sincere and pure, that your life is totally dedicated to Him, that you can be trusted because you are pursuing Him and not things—God will begin to pour out His blessings upon you. He will continue to pour them out on you more and more and more.

I know businessmen and businesswomen all over the country who were once striving to become wealthy. Their life's goal and ambition was simply to be a success. Their business became an obsession with them; it became their god.

Then they met the real God and made Jesus the Lord of their life. Suddenly, their attitude changed. They decided, "I'm not going to let this thing give me ulcers. I will do what is necessary to run this business, but I'm going to pursue God first." They started serving God, and God began to bless their business. God could trust them to take their increase and invest it wisely in the poor, in the needs of the saints, and in the ministry. So God keeps blessing their businesses, and those businesses keep growing.

Riches Are to Be Received—Not Pursued

Jesus said, "Assuredly, I say to you, there is no one who has left house or brothers or sisters or father or mother or wife or children or lands, for My sake and the gospel's, who shall not receive a hundredfold now in this time" (Mark 10:29–30).

Notice the key word in this verse: *receive*. Jesus was saying that the blessings of God are received, not pursued. If your desire is to become rich, you're headed for trouble. If you are in pursuit of riches, you're headed down the wrong road. Those who seek to pursue and please God receive wealth and riches and blessings. Such people don't strive after riches; riches are conferred upon them.

Once I got this truth in my spirit as a young man, I began to come out of bondage. My marriage got healed, and God delivered me financially and spiritually. He put my mind at ease and made a prosperous man out of me. I wasn't anybody special; I wasn't born under a lucky star. I just made up my mind to pursue God and His Word regardless of what anybody else thought. The Bible says, "Those who seek the LORD shall not lack any good thing" (Psalm 34:10).

Did I become a prosperous man overnight? No. Did I make mistakes along the way? Yes—but so did Abraham. As a young man, Abraham didn't know much about Jehovah God. It was in Genesis 12 that he set out to pursue God, trusting in His promises, but it wasn't until Genesis 17 that God revealed Himself to Abraham as El Shaddai, the all-sufficient One who provides and makes a way even in the face of impossibility.

Abraham had to learn about God. He didn't know anything about faith. The beautiful thing about Abraham's story is that he was just like us. He made mistakes, he failed, yet, God vindicated him when he consecrated his life to God and pursued Him. God called Abraham His friend and the father of faith. If Abraham, with all of his mistakes, could become the father of faith and the friend of God, surely you and I can become something in this world if we will pursue God as he did.

Abraham had to learn, and he did. The Bible says, "Now Abraham was old, well advanced in age; and the LORD had blessed Abraham in all things" (Genesis 24:1). Abraham was blessed in all things because he was obedient and faithfully pursued God throughout his life. Today, that same blessing is ours if we will be obedient and faithful.

When Jesus said those who pursued Him for the gospel's sake would receive a hundredfold, His disciples didn't learn everything they needed to know overnight. But, thank God, they learned it. It thrills me to read about Peter in the book of Acts. He acted just like Jesus; he did the same works Jesus had done, with the same results. God blessed Peter despite all of his blunders, mistakes, and failures. Why? Peter was willing to obey Jesus' instructions to "seek first the kingdom of God and His righteousness," knowing that "all these things" would be given to him (see Matthew 6:33).

Some people think God wants us to follow after righteousness, godliness, faith, love, patience, meekness—and be broke. It is certain that you will not be broke by following after righteousness, godliness, faith, love, patience, and meekness.

> Abraham was blessed in all things because he was obedient and faithfully pursued God throughout his life. Today, that same blessing is ours if we will be obedient and faithful.

The Word of God says, "Command those who are rich in this present age not to be haughty, nor to trust in uncertain riches, but in the living God who gives us richly all things to enjoy" (1 Timothy 6:17). Notice that riches are uncertain. In other words, you can't depend on money. About the time you think, "I have twenty thousand dollars; I can buy myself a car," they go up to thirty thousand.

I don't love money. I don't pursue riches and wealth. I follow after righteousness, peace, love, patience, meekness—and God gives me richly all things to enjoy. Does it sound like those who dedicate their lives to the pursuit of God will go without? No! God has said, "If you will serve Me, I will give you richly all things to enjoy." Jesus told His disciples the same thing when He said, "Do not worry about your life, what you will eat; nor about the body, what you will put on … your Father knows that you need these things. Do not fear, little flock, for it is your Father's good pleasure to give you the kingdom" (Luke 12:22, 30, 32). All we have to do is be willing to receive it.

When we make the decision to develop a lifestyle of pursuing God, our days of worrying about prosperity and material necessities are over—forever.

Chapter 10
A Call to Action

Mid-September marks the beginning of the fall season in North Carolina, making October a sensory experience for residents and visitors alike. The air is crisp, colors are vivid, and the smoky scent of a wood fire carried on the night breeze signals a change of season.

My wife, Carolyn, and I were ministering at a weeklong convention in Charlotte, and I'd had the sense even before we arrived that something special was going to take place in the meetings. At the same time, I knew something significant was also going to happen in my own life. I had no idea what it was, and I didn't try to figure it out. I just flowed with the Spirit of God as I enjoyed a sense of expectancy.

Carolyn and I had decided before we went to the convention that we were going to fast and stay in the presence of God every moment that we were not actually in the meeting. Very early each morning, I rose just to fellowship with God. When I would leave a meeting, I'd go right back to the hotel and stay in God's presence. This went on for almost the whole week, until Thursday afternoon.

When I finished preaching that day, Carolyn and I returned to our hotel suite. God had been dealing with me about some things, sharing with me about my own ministry and some new directions we were to take. Great things had happened in that convention, and I sensed a release in my spirit. So I told Carolyn, "I'm going to order some food and then just relax and rest before we leave for tonight's service."

She went into the bedroom to lie down and rest while I went into the living room, ordered room service, and sat down on the couch, immediately propping my feet upon the coffee table. I was just sitting there minding my own business, waiting for our food to arrive, when the tangible presence of the Lord filled the room. What happened next was something I'd never prayed would happen or that I'd even thought about happening: the Lord appeared to me.

His presence engulfed me; it filled the room. He said, "Son, my people are in financial famine, and I'm giving you the assignment to tell them how to get out." Then He began to reveal to me the pathway to deliverance for His people, some of which I've already shared in this book. But in addition to instructing me to teach God's people why He wants them to prosper, He charged me to tell the Body of Christ three specific things—all of which hinge upon our obedience to His Word.

First, He declared that He would command His blessing upon His people.

Second, He promised to rebuke the devourer on behalf of His people.

And third, He instructed the Body of Christ to sow in famine.

I don't know how long I was caught up in His presence. Although it seemed like hours, it may actually have been minutes. But when the Lord had finished talking with me, His presence—the Shekinah glory of God—was still so strong in the room that it awakened Carolyn. She ran into the room and asked, "What's happening in here?"

"The Lord just visited me," I answered.

We got so caught up in His glory that when our food arrived, sometime later, we couldn't even eat. I was so taken aback by what I'd experienced that I could hardly talk. Yet I sensed the urgency of what the Lord had told me: "Tell My people that I want them out of financial bondage."

That night I preached a portion of what the Lord had shared with me. Without a doubt, my life was changed that day, and the lives of thousands of others have been changed as well over the years. Every time I've shared this message, the testimonies have been phenomenal.

What the Lord spoke to me that day, which I've shared in churches, at conferences, on television, and in this book, isn't anything new. The material is all right there in the Word of God. The problem has been that many in the Body of Christ have either just ignored it or allowed carnally minded men and the world's system to deceive them into believing that what God's Word says won't work.

The job we've been called to do in these last days is tremendous and will demand financial freedom on our part. I want you to know that if you will open your heart and receive the following three messages the Lord gave me to tell you, you will come out of your financial famine and into the prosperity that is already yours.

#1: "I will command My blessing upon My people."

In His supernatural visitation with me, the Lord said, "I am going to divinely intervene on behalf of My people, and I am going to command My blessing upon them." This promise, of course, is written in the book of Deuteronomy, which says, "The LORD will command the blessing on you in your storehouses and in all to which you set your hand, and He will bless you in the land which the LORD God is giving you" (Deuteronomy 28:8).

I want you to realize how powerful the command of God is. When darkness was covering the earth, it took only a command of God to remove that darkness. When the earth was an empty, shapeless place existing without a purpose and all that could be found was a blanket of darkness resting on the surface, God commanded that there be light, and suddenly the light appeared (see Genesis 1:1-3). All God had to do to change the condition of this earth was to issue a command. It didn't take years. God spoke the word, and it came to pass.

God said, "I will command the blessing to come upon My people." All it would take to wipe out every financial debt is for God to say, "Financial debt, go!" God is capable of changing everything with just one word. That's how powerful He is.

> God is capable of changing everything with just one word. That's how powerful He is.

The psalmist wrote these words: "Let them praise the name of the LORD, for He commanded and they were created. He also established them forever and ever. He made a decree which shall not pass away" (Psalm 148:5–6). When God commands something, neither Satan, nor evil forces, nor even man can negate it. When God makes a decree, it stands. It is established. God is going to command His blessing upon you.

I am blessed because God has commanded His blessing upon me. Every time I turn around, I am being blessed. In fact, when He gave me this message for you that day in Charlotte, God told me, "Son, I'm going to use you as an example to prove to the Body of Christ that when I command the blessing upon My people, lack is a thing of the past." Since that moment, I have experienced some of the most tremendous financial miracles of my entire life. More than ever before, I have been able to give into good works and to families that are in need.

God spoke through the prophet Isaiah, saying, "Is My hand shortened at all that it cannot redeem? Or have I no power to deliver? Indeed with My rebuke I dry up the sea; I make the rivers a wilderness" (Isaiah 50:2).

Do you believe that God is just as capable of redeeming a people today as He was in the days of old? My God's hand is not shortened. He is still quite able to save us from our situation. Notice how He connects deliverance and redemption with words: "With My rebuke I dry up the sea." To reverse any situation, God only has to speak the word, and it is done. To experience the blessing of God in this manner, what we need is for God to simply speak. I want God talking to my money. Don't you? I want Him to speak to my finances.

My friend, we've listened to the world long enough. We've listened to the news reporters and commentators long enough. We've read *Time*,

Newsweek, U.S. News & World Report, and *The Wall Street Journal* long enough. Now let's find out what God has to say about our situation. He says, "I will command My blessings upon you. All I have to do is to speak to the sea and it will dry up." Anyone who is capable of doing that can surely change my economic condition without any trouble.

Do you believe God will do this for you? If you believe He will, then act like it. God can turn the tide of events with a word. One night Jesus proved that when His men were about to drown during a storm at sea (see Mark 4). In the account of this story, we see that to change those circumstances, He simply stood up in the boat and said, "Peace, be still!" (Mark 4:39). The waves stopped roaring, the wind ceased, and the sea calmed. The elements knew better than to disobey the voice of Almighty God. People ignore God; the elements don't.

Jesus spoke and the elements obeyed. The men with Him were astounded and asked themselves, "What manner of man is this?" (Mark 4:41 KJV). That is exactly what the world will be saying as God begins to command his blessings upon the Body of Christ.

Our God can do it! Our God will do it!

#2: "I will rebuke the devourer on behalf of My people."
The second thing the Lord told me that afternoon was, "Tell My people that, according to the word I spoke through Malachi, I will rebuke the devourer for their sakes."

Looking at Malachi 3:11–12, we read, "'And I will rebuke the devourer for your sakes, so that he will not destroy the fruit of your ground, nor shall the vine fail to bear fruit for you in the field,' says the LORD of hosts; 'and all nations will call you blessed, for you will be a delightful land,' says the LORD of hosts."

Satan cannot withstand God's rebuke. As believers, we have the authority to rebuke the devil. We typically don't rebuke him until we get totally fed up with what he's doing to us. We put up with his harassment until we get tired of it. Then, when we've taken all we can stand from him, we start rebuking him.

Do you know what the word *rebuke* means? "To express sharp, stern disapproval of; reprove; reprimand" (Dictionary.com). God said, "I'm going to command My blessings upon My people, and I'm going to rebuke the devourer for their sake. I'm going to talk to their finances and command blessings to come upon them. I'm going to take care of the adversary for them while those blessings are coming upon them. I'm going to address him very sharply. I'm going to reprimand him. He will no longer control their finances."

It excites me to know that God is rebuking the devil for me. When God rebukes, all hell trembles. The voice of Jesus is described like a multitude of rushing waters (see Revelation 1:15). Have you ever been to Niagara Falls? The roar of those falls can be heard for miles. That's how it is when God speaks.

Once, God spoke to Jesus from the skies and everybody thought it had thundered because of the weight of authority it carried (see John 12:29). When God says, "Satan, I rebuke you," all of hell and the principalities and powers of darkness reel under the force of that rebuke. As long as our God rebukes the devourer and commands blessings upon us, there is nothing the devil can do to keep us in bondage.

> As long as our God rebukes the devourer and commands blessings upon us, there is nothing the devil can do to keep us in bondage.

The word *devour* according to Merriam-Webster means "to eat up greedily or ravenously, to use up or destroy, to prey upon." You see, that's what the devil has been doing to our finances. He has been swallowing them up, and destroying them, to keep us in bondage.

But God has said, "I will rebuke the devourer for your sake."

#3: *"My people must sow in famine."*
The third thing the Lord spoke to me during His visitation was, "Son, if people will do what I'm telling them, I will give them the blessing of Isaac when he sowed in famine."

Even in divine intervention, there is always a condition that must be met. When God moves with a strong hand to deliver His people, there are conditions that must be met to receive that deliverance.

The Lord dealt with me about this. He said, "Son, I will command My blessing upon the people, and I will rebuke the devourer for their sakes. I will change their financial condition if they will do what I tell them to do."

When people are in famine and in financial bondage, they tend to hold back what they have. Fearing that they won't get any more, they look around at circumstances and get stingy. In times of famine, people start hoarding. They withhold, which is the worst thing they can do in that situation. Hoarding is totally contrary to the principles of God's Word.

Proverbs 11:24 says, "There is one who scatters, yet increases more; and there is one who withholds more than is right, but it leads to poverty." The New International Version says it this way: "One person gives freely, yet gains even more; another withholds unduly, but comes to poverty." A time of famine is not the time to hold on to the little bit you have. That is the time you need to sow. That's how you get out of famine—by sowing. Let's look at a story in Genesis 26:

> There was a famine in the land ...
>> Then the LORD appeared to [Isaac] and said: "Do not go down to Egypt [in other words, don't run away from the famine]; live in the land of which I shall tell you. Dwell in this land, and I will be with you and bless you; for to you and your descendents I give all these lands, and I will perform the oath which I swore to Abraham your father ... because Abraham obeyed My voice and kept My charge, My commandments, My statutes, and My laws" (Genesis 26:1–3, 5).

Notice that in the midst of famine, God told Isaac not to run or be afraid of it, but to stay where He had told him to dwell. He assured Isaac that He would be with him and take care of him even in the midst of the famine:

> Then Isaac sowed in that land, and reaped in the same year a hundredfold; and the LORD blessed him. The man began to prosper, and continued prospering until he became very prosperous; for he had possessions of flocks and possessions of herds and a great number of servants. So the Philistines envied him (Genesis 26:12–14).

Isaac didn't withhold in famine. He sowed in famine. He gave in famine.

God told me, "If My people will sow in the same spirit that Isaac sowed rather than withholding, I'll give them the blessing of Isaac." Then He said, "You start, Son, and I'll use you as an example."

I too was in famine at the time. I didn't have all I needed and was tired of it. That year had been one of the hardest periods financially for my ministry. We stood on the Word of God constantly. There was not one day that we could let up. We had to keep our faith against that mountain every day. It seemed that the more I received, the more it took to accomplish what God had called me to do. There was never enough.

That's when God said to me, "Are you fed up?"

I said, "Yes, I'm fed up."

He said, "I told you I'm going to command the blessing upon you and rebuke the devil for your sake. If you'll do what I'm telling you to do, if you'll sow in famine, I'll give you the blessing of Isaac—and in the same year a hundredfold."

Carolyn and I sat down together and took ten checks out of our ministry account, representing each of the ten major departments that were in famine. We wrote each check for a thousand dollars, a total of ten thousand dollars.

You might say, "You gave away ten thousand dollars? That doesn't sound like famine to me." It is when you need millions. Now, if you only need five dollars, then ten thousand is abundance, but when ten thousand doesn't come close to meeting your needs, then you are in famine.

Success to one person may not be success to someone else. Someone may say proudly, "I made a hundred thousand dollars this year," but to the person who normally makes five hundred thousand a year, that's famine.

The point is, I was in famine, and I was fed up with it. So Carolyn and I wrote out those ten checks for a thousand dollars each. We needed that ten thousand dollars desperately; but we sowed in famine, in obedience to God. We believed that God was going to command the blessing upon us and rebuke the devourer for our sake. The blessing of Isaac was going to come on us.

Then, because God had told me, "I will use you as an example to prove to the Body of Christ that I will do what I say," Carolyn and I took a thousand dollars from our own personal account, the last thousand we had, and sowed it in famine.

Within one week (not one year, but one week—seven days), God gave us an airplane worth $150,000, for which we owe not one thin dime! The next night I was given a check for $100,000 for the evangelistic ministry. Then I received another check for $10,000. But that wasn't all. At the end of the week, over a quarter of a million dollars had come in—all because we had sowed in famine.

Isaac sowed in famine and received a hundredfold return. God told me to tell you that He is going to give you the blessing of Isaac. You don't have to be a preacher for this to work for you. All you have to be is a believer.

I preached this message in a church in Oklahoma City. The people took it and acted upon it, sowing in famine, in their need. Later the pastor asked how many in the congregation had received financial miracles since they sowed in famine. Over 75 percent of his congregation stood to their feet! More than 75 percent of that church had received financial miracles because they had sowed in famine. This is a documented fact.

A woman called our office and said she'd been trying to sell her house for months. She got tired of it taking so long, so she sowed in famine. Her house sold the next day. That too is a documented fact.

I could go on and on. My files contain folders full of such documented testimonies. God is commanding His blessing upon His people.

Are you living in famine? Do you believe that God is no respecter of persons and that what He has done for me and for these I have mentioned, He will do for you?

In Exodus 35:4–5, we read these words:

> And Moses spoke to all the congregation of the children of Israel, saying, "This is the thing which the LORD

commanded, saying: 'Take from among you an offering to the LORD. Whoever is of a willing heart, let him bring it as an offering to the LORD.'"

God wants a voluntary act of faith on your part. He wants you to be of a willing heart. If you will sow out of your need for the spread of the gospel in these last days, God has promised that you will reap a bountiful harvest. Like I've already said, don't make this a one-time effort, but make it a lifestyle.

All God wants is an opportunity to command His blessings upon you and to rebuke the devourer for your sake. If you are of a willing heart and are ready to come out of your famine, then sow and sow and keep on sowing. Your freedom is at hand.

I received the Lord's call to action on behalf of the Body of Christ years ago in Charlotte, North Carolina. My assignment was to help get God's people out of financial famine and bondage, which I have been faithful to do since the Lord first spoke to me.

And the Lord has been faithful to me. He promised He would use me as an example to prove to the Body of Christ that when He commands His blessing, lack and poverty become things of the past.

Today, I am a prosperous man, not just materially but in all things that pertain to life and godliness. As a result of my obedience to God and His Word, God has used me to take the gospel literally into all the world. He has used me to be a blessing to others. And, right now, He is using me to deliver His call to action to you.

Won't you join me and thousands of others who have come to understand and operate in God's principle of prosperity? Together we can enjoy all of the benefits of His blessings as we make an impact for God on the lives of others, in the name of Jesus Christ.

After all, this is God's purpose for prosperity!

FURTHER RESOURCES FROM JERRY SAVELLE

JERRYSAVELLE.ORG

-Digital Magazine App
-On-Demand TV Programs
-Product Specials
-Video/Audio Downloads
-Tour Dates
-And Much More...

OTHER BOOKS BY JERRY SAVELLE

Called to Battle, Destined to Win
Every Day a Blessing Day
Free to be Yourself
If Satan Can't Steal Your Dreams. He Can't Control Your Destiny
If Satan Can't Steal Your Joy, He Can't Keep Your Goods
In the Footsteps of a Prophet
Increase God's Way
Living in the Fullness of the Blessing
No Boundaries
Prayer of Petition
Receive God's Best
The Established Heart
The Favor of God
The God of the Breakthrough Will Visit Your House
The Nature of Faith
Thoughts: The Battle Between Your Ears